EXTRAORDINARY PEOPLE OF THE

CIVIL RIGHTS MOVEMENT

by Sheila Hardy and P. Stephen Hardy

Children's Press®
A Division of Scholastic Inc.
New York   Toronto   London   Auckland   Sydney
Mexico City   New Delhi   Hong Kong
Danbury, Connecticut

This book is dedicated to our fathers, Nathaniel Edward Jackson and Lawrence Roy Hardy—men who did not stand for being "less than" anyone and who taught us the meaning of equality and pride.

Book production by Editorial Directions, Inc.

Library of Congress Cataloging-in-Publication Data
Hardy, Sheila Jackson.
  Extraordinary people of the civil rights movement / by Sheila Jackson Hardy & P. Stephen Hardy.
     p. cm. — (Extraordinary people)
  Includes bibliographical references and index.
  ISBN-10: 0-516-25461-8 (lib. bdg.)
           0-516-29847-X (pbk.)
  ISBN-13: 978-0-516-25461-6 (lib. bdg.)
           978-0-516-29847-4 (pbk.)
  1. African American civil rights workers—Biography—Juvenile literature. 2. Civil rights workers—United States—Biography—Juvenile literature. 3. African Americans—Civil rights—History--20th century—Juvenile literature. 4. Civil rights movements—United States—History—20th century—Juvenile literature. 5. United States—Race relations—History—20th century—Juvenile literature. I. Hardy, P. Stephen. II. Title. III. Series.
  E185.96.H332 2006
  323.092'396073–dc22   2005037533

CONTENTS

51
Thurgood Marshall
(1908–1993)
U.S. Supreme Court Justice

55
Clarence Mitchell Jr.
(1911–1984)
Lawyer and Lobbyist

59
Amzie Moore
(1911–1982)
Civil Rights Activist,
Mississippi

63
Isaiah DeQuincey Newman
(1911–1985)
Civil Rights Activist,
South Carolina

66
Bayard Taylor Rustin
(1912–1987)
Cofounder of the SCLC

70
Daisy Bates
(1914–1999)
Friend and Adviser to
the Little Rock Nine

75
Fannie Lou Hamer
(1917–1977)
Civil Rights Activist and
Cofounder of the MFDP

79
James Leonard Farmer Jr.
(1920–1999)
Civil Rights Leader, Cofounder
of CORE

84
Dr. Joseph Lowery
(1921–)
Civil Rights Activist, Alabama

87
Constance Baker Motley
(1921–2005)
Attorney, Politician,
Federal Judge

90
Avon Nyanza Williams Jr.
(1921–1994)
Attorney

94
Fred Lee Shuttlesworth
(1922 –)
Civil Rights Leader,
Cofounder of the SCLC

97
Ernest C. Withers
(1922–)
Photographer

100
Aaron Henry
(1922–1997)
Civil Rights Leader,
Mississippi

104
Charles Evers
(1922–)
Civil Rights Activist,
Mississippi

107

Mae Bertha Carter
(1923–1999)
Civil Rights Activist,
Mississippi

111

Cordy Tindell Vivian
(1924–)
Civil Rights Activist,
Tennessee

114

Medgar Evers
(1925–1963)
Civil Rights Leader

119

**Malcolm Little, a.k.a. Malcolm
X, El Hajj Malik El Shabazz**
(1925–1965)
Civil Rights Leader

124

Ralph Abernathy
(1926–1990)
Civil Rights Leader

127

Hosea Williams
(1926–2000)
Civil Rights Activist
and Organizer

131

**Harold "Harry"
George Belafonte Jr.**
(1927–)
Singer, Actor, Producer,
Activist, and Humanitarian

135

Coretta Scott King
(1927–2006)
First Lady of the
Civil Rights Movement

139

James Lawson
(1928–)
Civil Rights Leader

143

Dr. Martin Luther King Jr.
(1929–1968)
Civil Rights Leader

149

Dorothy Foreman Cotton
(c. 1931–)
Civil Rights Leader,
Educator

152

**Richard "Dick"
Claxton Gregory**
(1932–)
Comedian, Civil Rights
Activist, Author

156

Andrew Jackson Young Jr.
(1932–)
Civil Rights Leader

159

Unita Blackwell
(1933–)
Civil Rights Leader,
Mississippi

163

Walter Fauntroy
(1933–)
Civil Rights Activist
and Lobbyist

167

James Meredith
(1933–)
Civil Rights Activist, Mississippi

171

Myrlie Evers-Williams
(1933–)
Civil Rights Leader

174

Robert "Bob" Moses
(1935–)
Civil Rights Activist,
Organizer, and Educator

177

Marion Shepilov Barry Jr.
(1936–)
Civil Rights Leader,
Politician

181

Dr. James Luther Bevel
(1936–)
Civil Rights Leader

186

Diane Nash
(1938–)
Civil Rights Activist,
Tennessee

190

Horace Julian Bond
(1940–)
Civil Rights Leader
and Journalist

194

John R. Lewis
(1940–)
Civil Rights Leader,
Politician

198

James Zwerg
(1940–)
Civil Rights Activist

202

**Stokely Carmichael, a.k.a.
Kwame Toure**
(1941–1998)
Civil Rights Leader

206

Jesse Louis Jackson Sr.
(1941–)
Civil Rights Leader, Politician

210

Emmett Till
(1941–1955)
Innocent Victim

214

Dr. James Edward Orange
(1942–)
Civil Rights Activist, Alabama

217

Dr. Bernice Johnson Reagon
(1942–)
Civil Rights Activist, Singer,
Composer, and Scholar

221

**The Women of the
Montgomery Bus Boycott**
(1955)
Jo Ann Robinson, Claudette
Colvin, and Rosa Parks

INTRODUCTION

For the purposes of this book, we have defined the period known as the civil rights movement as the years from 1954 to 1968. It begins with U.S. Supreme Court decision *Brown v. Board of Education* and ends with Martin Luther King Jr.'s Poor People's Campaign. Although we have focused on the events of those years, there were many important civil rights activities before 1954, and there have been many since 1968.

In the late 1920s, the sleeping-car porters with the Pullman Company wanted better working conditions and higher wages. A. Philip Randolph led the first African American labor union, which was a union of sleeping-car porters. The union's motto, "Fight or Be Slaves," galvanized the workers, who successfully negotiated the first contract ever made between an African American union and a large industrialized company.

By 1940, there was a threat of war in the United States, but the majority of union jobs available in factories and weapons plants were not open to African Americans. That year Randolph organized the first march on Washington for civil rights. The mere threat of such a large protest prompted President Franklin Delano Roosevelt to sign an executive order. The order called for an end to discrimination based on creed, color, or national origin in the employment of workers in defense industries and government. The newly created Fair Employment Practices Committee (FEPC) began to investigate claims of racial discrimination. Randolph's march was ultimately canceled because its goals had been reached. African Americans learned that by coming together, they had

Many African American soldiers fought bravely for the United States and freedom during World War II, but returned home to face ongoing racial discrimination.

collective power to change national policy—a valuable lesson in nonviolent resistance that later would define the events of the 1950s and 1960s.

Just as it takes a spark to light a fire, several incidents set off the level of activism that became known as the civil rights movement. The first sit-in took place eighteen years before the famous sit-ins at the lunch counters at Woolworth's department store in Greensboro, North Carolina. In 1942, James Farmer and George Hauser stopped for coffee and doughnuts at Jack Spratt's Coffee Shop in Chicago. The two men, along with other members of the Committee on Racial Equality (later the Congress of Racial Equality), successfully convinced Jack Spratt's to open its doors to both black and white customers.

During World War II, tens of thousands of African American soldiers answered the call to "make the world safe for democracy." In Europe, these soldiers were respected and embraced as equals. But when they returned home, these men who had fought for freedom abroad were lynched, brutalized, sent to the backs of buses, and denied the right to vote. Having risked their lives fighting for democracy, they were unwilling to accept these harsh conditions. They were ready to join the freedom movement that was already slowly gaining momentum.

On trains that traveled from Northern to Southern states, white and black passengers rode in separate sections, with blacks at the back of the cars. In 1946, the U.S. Supreme Court's decision in *Morgan v. The Commonwealth of Virginia* made segregation on interstate travel unconstitutional. In 1947, activists tested the new law by attempting to integrate trains and buses that were traveling from state to state. Participants in this first Freedom Ride, then called the Journey of Reconciliation, were arrested, jailed, and sentenced to work on a chain gang. For eight years, riders documented their experiences. The National Association for the Advancement of Colored People (NAACP) provided lawyers to defend the protesters whenever needed. These symbolic rides showed Southern segregationists that people were willing to be jailed for the cause of freedom.

There are key figures in the civil rights movement, such as Dr. Martin Luther King Jr., who brought major issues to national attention. There were also many other people whose contributions to the movement are often overlooked in history books. They have remained invisible—until now.

Our goal is to share many of the untold stories of those who risked their lives, and in some cases lost them, to fight against discrimination in order to change America for the better. We hope their stories will inspire and encourage others.

TIMELINE OF KEY EVENTS

1954–1968

1954

The Supreme Court rules in favor of *Brown v. Board of Education* and orders the desegregation of public schools.

Students protest at Howard University.

1955

Fourteen-year-old Emmett Till is murdered in Money, Mississippi.

Southerners opposing desegregation form the White Citizens' Council, a group committed to making it difficult for blacks to find work or get bank loans.

Rosa Parks is arrested in Montgomery, Alabama, for refusing to give up her seat on a bus to a white passenger.

The Montgomery Bus Boycott tests the Supreme Court's ruling to integrate interstate travel.

1956

Congressmen from the Southern states sign the Southern Manifesto, opposing the Supreme Court's ruling in *Brown v. Board of Education.*

The home of Dr. Martin Luther King Jr. is firebombed.

Martin Luther King Jr. rides a bus in Montgomery.

1957

The Southern Christian Leadership Conference (SCLC), an organization of church leaders and others working for civil rights, is founded. Martin Luther King Jr. is named its president and Ella Baker its executive director.

Nine courageous African American teenagers, known as the Little Rock Nine, integrate a high school in Little Rock, Arkansas, under the guidance of Daisy Lee Gatson Bates.

The federal government attempts to close the Highlander Folk School in Monteagle, Tennessee. The civil rights training center provided workshops on labor unions, workers' rights, and race relations.

1960

John Fitzgerald Kennedy is elected president of the United States, with Lyndon Baines Johnson as his vice president.

Students hold sit-ins at the lunch counter at Woolworth's department store in Greensboro, North Carolina, which lead to sit-ins at counters in Nashville, Tennessee, and other parts of the South.

The Student Nonviolent Coordinating Committee (SNCC), which is based on the peaceful principles of Indian leader Mohandas Gandhi, is founded.

1961

Freedom Riders sit beside a bus that was burned by a mob that attacked it on the highway.

White and black activists take a series of Freedom Rides on buses and trains through the South to challenge the Supreme Court's ruling against segregated travel.

The Albany Movement forms in Albany, Georgia, to organize activists in protests against segregation. This results in the arrests of many important civil rights leaders, including Ralph Abernathy and Martin Luther King Jr.

1962

James Meredith becomes the first African American to attend the University of Mississippi.

The Council of Federated Organizations (COFO) is founded, uniting several civil rights organizations in efforts to register voters throughout the South.

James Meredith at the University of Mississippi

1963

Governor George Wallace tries to prevent African Americans from attending the University of Alabama. President John F. Kennedy orders the National Guard to escort the students to school.

Medgar Evers, an officer of the NAACP who is investigating the murder of Emmett Till, is shot and killed.

On August 28, an estimated quarter million civil rights activists participate in the March on Washington for Jobs and Freedom.

Four young girls are killed when a church in Birmingham, Alabama, is bombed.

President John F. Kennedy is assassinated.

1964

The Twenty-Fourth Amendment to the U.S. Constitution is approved, abolishing the voting fees known as poll taxes. Poll taxes kept African Americans in the South from exercising their right to vote.

The Mississippi Freedom Democratic Party (MFDP) forms to challenge the all-white Democratic Party in Mississippi.

In the project known as Freedom Summer, about one thousand predominately white volunteers travel to Mississippi to help register African Americans to vote, to provide legal aid, and to establish health clinics.

Fannie Lou Hamer speaks at the Democratic National Convention and exposes the brutal injustices of the South to the world.

1964 (CONTINUED)

Three civil rights workers—two white men and one black—disappear in Mississippi. President Lyndon B. Johnson sends two hundred troops to search for them.

James Meredith starts a solitary March Against Fear from Memphis, Tennessee, to Jackson, Mississippi. He is forced to stop when a sniper wounds him, and other civil rights activists complete the march in his honor.

President Lyndon B. Johnson signs the Civil Rights Act of 1964, outlawing discrimination and segregation in public places and requiring employers to provide equal employment opportunities to all races.

Martin Luther King Jr. is awarded the Nobel Peace Prize.

1965

Malcolm X

Radical black leader Malcolm X is assassinated in New York.

On what is now known as Bloody Sunday, peaceful protesters are attacked by police during a march from Selma, Alabama, to the state capitol in Montgomery.

President Lyndon B. Johnson signs the Voting Rights Act of 1965, which abolishes all restrictions that deny people the right to vote.

1966

Stokely Carmichael launches his Black Power movement as an alternative to nonviolent protest.

Stokely Carmichael (right)

1968

Three African American students in Orangeburg, South Carolina, are killed and others are wounded in what would become known as the Orangeburg Massacre.

Sanitation workers in Tennessee lead the Memphis sanitation workers' strike, a successful, sixty-five-day campaign for better working conditions.

Martin Luther King Jr. is assassinated on the balcony of his motel room in Memphis, Tennessee, on April 4.

Rev. Ralph Abernathy carries out Martin Luther King Jr.'s plans for the Poor People's Campaign and leads thousands of people to Washington, D.C., to call attention to the problems of poor Americans of all races.

ASA PHILIP RANDOLPH
Union Leader and Organizer
(1889–1979)

Freedom is never granted, it is won. Justice is never given; it is exacted and the struggle must be continuous.

A. Philip Randolph was the single greatest architect of the civil rights movement in America. He forced the organized labor movement to accept blacks into their unions, which led to the formation of a black middle class in America.

Randolph was born on April 15, 1889, in Crescent City, Florida. He attended the Cookman Institute in East Jacksonville, Florida, and graduated in 1907 as class valedictorian. W. E. B. Du Bois's book *The Souls of Black Folk* convinced young Randolph that the most important thing he could do was to fight for social equality. So he turned his attention to politics, economics, and philosophy.

Randolph attended City College in New York City at night and worked odd jobs during the day. At that time, Randolph and many black Americans believed democracy in the United States had failed to live up to its promise of freedom and equality for all. He joined the Socialist Party. Socialists believe that the common person should have more of a say in how the nation and businesses are run.

In 1917, Randolph and his friend Chandler Owen, a sociology student at Columbia University, started a magazine called the *Messenger*. Topics included politics, union news, and literary criticism by important African Americans, such as Paul Robeson and Claude McKay. In 1918, Randolph and Owen were arrested and charged with treason for their antiwar views. The U.S. attorney general called them the "most dangerous Negroes in the United States."

In those days, people traveled long distances by train, and passengers would sleep in specially designed sleeping cars. George Pullman, the inventor of the sleeping car, hired black men to work as porters on the cars. There were so few jobs open to black men that Pullman was able to force them to work long hours for low pay. By the 1930s, as many as one hundred thousand passengers slept in Pullman cars on any given night. Pullman's company was one of the most powerful businesses in the nation.

In 1925, a group of sleeping-car porters told Randolph they wanted to form an official union to protect their rights. The porters needed a leader who the company could not simply threaten or fire. The men asked Randolph for help, and he accepted. Over the next twelve years, Randolph forged a nationally recognized union, called the Brotherhood of Sleeping Car Porters (BSCP), to bargain for fair treatment of the workers. Pullman did everything he could to block the union. He hired spies, fired workers who supported the union efforts, and hired people to beat up and threaten union workers. On three occasions, Pullman offered Randolph money to stop his work with the union.

In 1935, President Franklin D. Roosevelt's New Deal legislation guaranteed workers the right to organize and required companies to negotiate with unions. Two years later, Randolph and the porters won a contract agreement with the Pullman Company. It was the first time in American history that organized black workers had won their case against a large industrial corporation.

In the 1940s and 1950s, Randolph turned his attention to the rising number of African Americans who were unemployed, even while the number of jobs in the war industry was increasing. Thousands of good-paying union jobs were opening up in factories and weapons plants—but African Americans were not able to get them. Randolph decided that it was time for mass action to demand change. He organized "10,000 loyal Negro American citizens" in a march to Washington, D.C., to insist on equal treatment. Officials in Washington and conservative black leaders panicked and tried to convince him not to go through with the march. The more they pressured him to call it off, the harder Randolph worked to increase the number of marchers who would participate.

On June 25, 1941, only six days before the march was scheduled to take place, Roosevelt signed an executive order that forbid "discrimination in the employment of workers in defense industries or government because of race, creed, color or national origin." Still, Randolph was not sure the order would actually be enforced. Roosevelt then created the Fair Employment Practices Committee (FEPC) to investigate claims of racial discrimination, so Randolph called off the march. By the end of 1944, nearly two million African Americans were working in defense industries. Those federal jobs signaled the beginning of the formation of a large black middle class in America.

Randolph's fight for equality was not over. He also demanded an end to segregation of black and white servicemen in the armed forces. He formed the League for Nonviolent Civil Disobedience against Military Segregation. He called on young men of all races to refuse to register for the military draft or to refuse to serve if called.

By now, Harry Truman was president, and he was worried about the effects of this mass protest. He also needed the black vote to win reelection. On July 26, 1948, Truman signed an executive order that commanded an end to military segregation "as quickly as possible." Again, Randolph had achieved his goal and called off his plan for protest.

The recession of the 1950s brought harsh economic times for blacks. By 1962, the African American unemployment rate was twice that of the white unemployment rate. The lack of progress in gaining equal rights left many in the black community feeling dissatisfied and betrayed. Randolph believed the time had come to march on Washington for "jobs and freedom." He called together black leaders to take action, but now, at age seventy-four, Randolph felt he was too old to organize it himself. He appointed Bayard Rustin to organize the march, which took place on August 28, 1963. Never before had so many citizens assembled in peace to send a message to their government. Estimates of the crowd's size varied between 250,000 and 400,000.

In 1964, President Lyndon Johnson awarded Randolph the Presidential Medal of Freedom. Four years later, Randolph was named president of the A. Philip Randolph Institute, which was formed to promote trade unions in the black community.

Asa Philip Randolph understood that no one could truly be free without having the means to support his or her family. He brought the American promise of freedom and justice to workers by showing them the power that people have when they stand up for their rights.

CHARLES HAMILTON HOUSTON

CHIEF LEGAL COUNSEL FOR THE NAACP
(1895–1950)

I made up my mind that if I got through this war I would study law and use my time fighting for men who could not strike back.

Charles Hamilton Houston was born on September 3, 1895, in Washington, D.C. He was valedictorian of his high school class, and in 1911, he enrolled at Amherst College in Massachusetts, where he graduated Phi Beta Kappa. Houston wanted to follow in the tradition of his father and become a lawyer, but World War I was under way, and Houston was drafted into the U.S. Army. The injustice he experienced while serving as an African American officer strengthened his conviction to pursue a career in law.

In 1919, Houston enrolled in Harvard Law School, where he served as the first African American editor of the *Harvard*

Law Review. After graduation, he attended the University of Madrid in Spain and completed postdoctoral studies in law. While in Madrid, he applied for a faculty appointment at the historically black Howard University Law School in his home city of Washington, D.C.

Houston believed that African Americans needed strong legal representation if they were ever to enjoy their rights. In 1929, he was appointed vice dean of Howard's Law School, with the mandate to turn the school around. Houston knew that a lawyer needed a firm grasp of constitutional law to argue cases of civil rights—but at that time, only a few African American lawyers were trained in this area of the law.

Judges ridiculed Howard law graduates because of their poor presentations in the courtroom, and the school's law program was not accredited by the American Bar Association. Houston knew that Howard needed a full-time, accredited program that would better prepare students to practice law. He discontinued the school's night school classes because he believed that a person serious about becoming a lawyer should attend classes full-time.

Houston also raised the requirements for acceptance into the school and searched the country for the brightest students he could find. He made sure all his students understood that they would be competing against extremely well-trained white lawyers and had to be ready for the challenge. He also instilled in them his belief that the only work that was worthy of a Howard lawyer was work that improved the conditions of the poor and unprotected. Howard student Edward Lovett later recalled, "Whether it was equity or contracts or pleadings, stress was placed on learning what our rights were under the constitution and statutes." One of Houston's students was Thurgood Marshall, who later became a U.S. Supreme Court justice.

The 1896 U.S. Supreme Court case *Plessy v. Ferguson* was one of the most damaging to the civil rights of African Americans. In its ruling, the

Supreme Court established the legal segregation of blacks and whites under the false policy of "separate but equal." This ruling stated that all Americans were guaranteed access to public accommodations—but not necessarily the same accommodations. So as long as blacks had public accommodations of some sort—however bad they might be—whites could have separate accommodations of their own. This ruling affected all aspects of society, including schools and universities.

In 1933, Nathan Ross Margold, a white Harvard-trained lawyer for the National Association for the Advancement of Colored People (NAACP), crafted a legal strategy to end the segregation of blacks and whites in schools. His strategy was known as the Margold Report, and in it, he pointed out the weaknesses of the *Plessy* decision.

In 1935, the NAACP asked Houston to take on the fight against segregation. He worked seven days a week and often seventeen to eighteen hours a day to create a detailed, long-range strategy for a series of cases that would overturn the *Plessy* case.

Houston planned to challenge segregation in professional and graduate schools first. He believed that desegregation in those settings would be less threatening to the general public and that the case would more acceptable to the judges. He would then work his way through cases that involved colleges, high schools, and, finally, elementary schools. Houston's first victory was a case brought to him by his former student Thurgood Marshall. In June 1935, the two men tried the case of *Murray v. The University of Maryland Law School*. The all-white school had denied Donald Murray admission because he was black.

Houston and Marshall were a potent combination. Marshall could charm attorneys with a joke or two and pull valuable information from witnesses in casual conversation. Houston's eye for detail and command of constitutional law helped them make solid arguments. The team won the case based on the fact that a black citizen of the state who wished to study law and practice in Maryland was constitutionally guaranteed the right to do so. There were no law schools for blacks in Maryland, and the state could not simply send the student to school in another state.

In 1936, the case of *Gaines v. The University of Missouri Law School* helped Houston and Marshall establish that states had to provide an equal education for their black and white citizens. This victory opened the door to lawsuits involving other public facilities, such as libraries, swimming pools, parks, and hospitals, all of which were, at that time, segregated in the South.

In 1940, Houston returned to his father's law firm, and Marshall replaced him as lead counsel for the NAACP. The NAACP later created a separate organization called the NAACP Legal Defense and Educational Fund, which Marshall directed.

When Houston died at the young age of fifty-four, a book was lying by his hospital bed. In it were a few final words written for his young son: "Tell Bo I did not run out on him but went down fighting that he might have better and broader opportunities than I had without prejudice or bias operating against him, and that in any fight some fall."

SEPTIMA POINSETTE CLARK

CIVIL RIGHTS ACTIVIST AND EDUCATOR

(1898–1987)

I never felt that getting angry would do you any good other than hurt your own digestion—keep you from eating, which I liked to do.

Septima Poinsette Clark, who is sometimes known as the Queen Mother of the Civil Rights Movement, was born on May 3, 1898, in Charleston, South Carolina. Her father was a former slave and her mother a free-born woman from Haiti. Although at that time, African Americans had limited opportunities for learning how to read and write, Clark's parents made sure that all of their children had an education.

The public high schools in Charleston would not accept African American children, so Clark attended Avery Institute, a private school run by missionaries. Tuition was $1.50 per month, which was a lot of money in the early 1900s. Clark worked as a babysitter and a maid to help pay for her schooling.

With little more than high-school education, Clark began her career as a teacher. She traveled by boat daily to Johns Island, a remote spot off the coast of South Carolina, where a community of African Americans known as the Gullah Islanders lived. She worked with another teacher to educate 132 children, ranging from first through eighth grades. Clark also taught several adults.

In 1918, Clark returned to Charleston to teach at her alma mater, the Avery Institute. She joined African American teachers in their fight to teach in African American public schools, a battle they won in 1920. Shortly afterward, Clark married and moved to North Carolina, where she attended North Carolina Agricultural and Technical State University. A few years later, her husband died, and Clark and her young son returned home to Charleston. She resumed teaching on Johns Island, but the rural conditions were too harsh for her son, so she sent him back to North Carolina to live with his grandparents. In 1929, she was offered a teaching job at Benedict College in Columbia, South Carolina, where she had been taking classes every summer.

Clark quickly became part of the social and political organizations in Columbia. It was more than twenty-five years before the widespread sit-ins, boycotts, and protests for civil rights would begin, and many African Americans at the time were afraid to speak out against injustice. Clark joined the NAACP to fight alongside Thurgood Marshall for the right of African American teachers to receive pay equal to that of white teachers. In 1942, with new legislation, African American teachers saw a huge pay increase, and Clark's salary tripled.

Clark completed a bachelor's degree in 1942 and went on to earn a master's degree from Hampton Institute in 1946. In 1954, after the landmark U.S. Supreme Court decision *Brown v. Board of Education*, which desegregated public schools, Southern politicians wanted to tighten the rein on African American teachers. The South Carolina legislature passed a law to prohibit public employees from joining the NAACP or any civil rights organization. Clark refused to give up her membership and was dismissed without a pension.

Clark turned misfortune into opportunity. She took a position with the Highlander Folk School in Monteagle, Tennessee. Highlander was a training ground for civil rights activists and a haven for people of all races interested in peace and empowerment. There people learned how to read and write so they could understand the Constitution. They also learned about labor unions, workers' rights, and nonviolent protests, and gained practical survival skills. Clark added her own teaching model, which helped adults master math and reading by solving everyday problems. As director of workshops, Clark educated and inspired many people who later became important civil rights leaders, such as Rosa Parks, James Bevel, John Lewis, and Diane Nash.

In 1954, Esau Jenkins came to Highlander and shared the story about the people of Johns Island. Jenkins was a bus driver on a route from the island to Charleston and back again. Many passengers asked him to teach them to read and write so they could study the Constitution, pass the literacy test, and vote.

Jenkins's story spurred an idea that Clark had already set in motion—citizenship schools. Jenkins, Clark, and Clark's cousin Bernice Robinson created a working model that enabled more than six hundred African Americans to become registered voters. South Carolina and Tennessee politicians shut down the Highlander School in 1959—but Clark continued her work through the Southern Christian Leadership Conference (SCLC), training teachers and establishing citizenship schools throughout the South. The citizenship schools helped to register more than two million African American voters in the South.

In 1964, Clark accompanied Dr. Martin Luther King Jr. to Oslo, Norway, where he accepted the Nobel Peace Prize. King described Clark as a huge influence on his philosophy of nonviolence and gave her credit for much of the success of the civil rights movement.

In 1970, Clark retired from the SCLC. She returned to Charleston and served two terms on the school board. In 1976, she finally received partial payment of her long-denied pension from her years as a schoolteacher in Charleston, and in 1981, she received eight years of back pay from the state of South Carolina.

During the civil rights movement, women activists received little or no credit for their contributions. At the first convention of the National Organization for Women in 1958, Clark encouraged women to speak out against sexism, which she called a major weakness of the civil rights movement. During the 1970s and 1980s, Clark organized day-care centers for single moms and championed women's rights and human rights with her inspirational speeches and experiences.

Clark has been honored with presidential awards and honorary degrees. In 1987, her biography, *Ready from Within,* won the American Book Award. "I believe unconditionally in the ability of people to respond when they are told the truth," she once said. "We need to be taught to study rather than to believe, to inquire rather than to affirm." Clark herself taught thousands, who in turn went on to teach millions.

ZEPHANIAH ALEXANDER LOOBY

ATTORNEY

(1899–1972)

I am not the leader of the Negro people. The people know where they want to go. I am merely part of a team that helps them choose the right road.

Zephaniah Alexander Looby was born on April 8, 1899, on the Caribbean island of Antigua, in the British West Indies. He was just a little boy when his mother died, and his father died when Looby was a teenager. He struggled for years to survive on his own. During those hard times, he would sit for hours in the local courtroom and listen to the judges and lawyers, dreaming of one day becoming a lawyer himself.

Determined to find a better life, Looby took a job on a whaling ship bound for the United States. When the ship docked at New Bedford, Massachusetts, he went ashore. He worked odd jobs—in a bakery, yarn mill, and restaurant—but he never forgot his dream. To educate himself, he read at every opportunity, and he was later accepted at Howard University in Washington, D.C. After graduation, he enrolled in Columbia University and received his law degree in 1925. The next year, he earned a doctorate of law from New York University.

Those were fantastic achievements for a young man without a formal grade-school education, and even more so for a black person in those days. Looby was hired by Fisk University in Nashville, Tennessee, as an associate professor of economics. He passed the Tennessee state bar exam and set up his law practice in 1928, turning his attention to civil rights cases.

There were only a few black lawyers in the South during the 1930s, so when the National Association for the Advancement of Colored People (NAACP) needed lawyers to help them in their civil rights lawsuits, Looby was high on their list.

Looby's first big case was in 1946 when two World War II veterans, one white and the other black, had an argument that resulted in a fistfight. Soon after, a white mob formed to attack black businesses and residential areas in Columbia, Tennessee. African American residents armed themselves and warned the whites to stay out of their neighborhood.

On the night of February 25, 1946, four police officers ignored the residents' warnings and were shot and wounded. Angry whites then attacked the neighborhood. The National Guard was called in to restore order, and twenty-five African Americans were arrested. At their trial, all the jury members were white, and the lawyers had to endure constant threats against their lives, but Looby and the others cleared all but two of the men.

By the close of the 1940s, some people referred to Looby as Mr. Civil Rights. Although attorneys Charles Hamilton Houston and Thurgood Marshall directed the efforts of the NAACP's legal strategy nationally, they relied heavily on state attorneys to help them. From their base in Nashville,

Z. Alexander Looby and his partner, Avon Williams, championed the rights of African Americans across Tennessee.

The team of Looby and Williams also were the legal advisers for the Reverend Kelly Miller Smith during the 1950s and 1960s. Smith headed the Nashville Christian Leadership Conference (NCLC), the local arm of the Southern Christian Leadership Conference. Looby and Williams worked on voter registration and the desegregation of downtown restaurants. They also provided advice and legal representation for the organizers of student sit-ins.

Looby's home after it was bombed by racists on April 19, 1960

Students staged sit-ins as a form of protest to force restaurants to do away with segregated seating. White and black students would enter a restaurant, and the white students would sit in the "colored-only" section and the black students would sit in the "whites only" section. The students would refuse to leave until they received service or until the police came to arrest them for breaking the segregation laws. When the police took the students away, another group of students would take their seats and repeat the action. The NAACP's Legal Defense and Educational Fund provided those who were arrested with lawyers, who would bail the students out of jail and represent them in court. Looby and Williams kept very busy with this kind of work, which they often did for free.

In April 1960, racists tried to kill Looby and his family with a bomb, which damaged his home and the homes of his neighbors. The failed attempt to kill Looby actually served to strengthen his position as a civil rights leader and brought more people into the cause for civil rights. Telegrams and letters of sympathy, some with checks, poured in from twenty different states and from places as far away as Nigeria, Kenya, and Switzerland.

The day after the bombing, at a gathering at Fisk University where Dr. Martin Luther King Jr. was to speak, the audience of four thousand gave Looby a standing ovation that lasted so long it moved him to tears.

Thanks to the efforts of Looby, Williams, the NCLC, students, and others, seven restaurants were desegregated in Nashville. It was the first major Southern city to make this huge step toward the integration of whites and blacks in public settings.

Looby and Williams won many other cases involving employment discrimination, unfair housing practices, and segregation of public schools. The team was responsible for the successful merger of the all-white downtown University of Tennessee–Nashville and the historically black Tennessee State University. This event marked the first time in American history that a major white university joined with an African American institution. The African American faculty and leadership retained control of the new school.

In 1951, Looby won a seat on Nashville's city council, which gave him a voice in city government. He kept that position until failing health forced him to step down in 1971. He also served on the board of directors for the NAACP from 1953 to 1954 and again from 1956 to 1962.

Although Looby often endured verbal threats and violent, racist attacks during his long career, he was also rewarded with high praise. In 1949, an anonymous writer for Nashville's *Church Service Directory and News Journal* wrote, "In our midst we are fortunate to have one whose civil interest and marked ability rates him among the Nation's leading citizens. He has no peers as a race man and his victories as an attorney are inspiring to a group struggling to find its place in the sun."

EDGAR DANIEL NIXON

CIVIL RIGHTS ACTIVIST, ALABAMA
(1899–1987)

Fifty thousand people rose up and caught hold to the Cradle of the Confederacy and began to rock it 'til the Jim Crow rockers began to reel and the segregated slats began to fall out.

Edgar Daniel "E. D." Nixon was born on July 12, 1899. He worked as a Pullman porter on the Montgomery–Chicago route and got his start in the civil rights movement as a union organizer for the Brotherhood of Sleeping Car Porters (BSCP), the first African American union. Nixon campaigned for voting rights during the late 1930s and the 1940s. The persuasive Alabama native led a group of more than 750 men in a march to the Montgomery Courthouse, where they attempted to register to vote.

Nixon was determined to change the harsh racial climate of his segregated

Nixon (second from left) arrives at court with Rosa Parks in 1956.

Southern hometown. He worked tirelessly as president of the local chapter of the National Association for the Advancement of Colored People (NAACP), the Montgomery Welfare League, and the Montgomery Voter's League. He also worked with members of the African American community when they needed help in their dealings with politicians, the police, and other public servants.

Rosa Parks contacted Nixon when she was arrested by police for her refusal to give up her seat on the bus to a white man. He handled everything, from the arrangements for bail to her legal representation. He informed reporter Joe Azbell of the *Montgomery Advertiser* that a bus boycott was in the planning stages. The purpose of the boycott was to support the rights of African American working people to have equal access to public transportation. Nixon requested the story run on the front page.

Nixon also called the new pastor in town—Dr. Martin Luther King Jr.—and asked him to host a meeting of ministers to organize support for the boycott. Before King even agreed, Nixon invited the ministers to his Dexter Avenue Church. After the meeting, Nixon sat down with Rev. Ralph Abernathy and Rev. E. N. French to develop plans for a new organization, called the Montgomery Improvement Association (MIA), and to nominate Dr. King as its president.

After the first successful day of the boycott, Nixon urged the ministers to continue the one-day protest. He challenged them to stand up for the workers who relied on bus transportation, pointing out that 63 percent of African American women in Montgomery worked as washerwomen. "What's the matter with you people?" Nixon said. "Here you been living off the sweat of these washerwomen all these years and you have never done anything for them. Now you have a chance to pay them back, and you're too damn scared to stand on your feet and be counted." White segregationists bombed Nixon's home on February 1, 1956, although no one was harmed.

Nixon was one of the only members of the MIA who was not a clergyman, and the men often disagreed. Nixon also began to resent that the media focused its attention on the nationally known King and Abernathy, while he and other local activists who had struggled for years before the young ministers got involved were ignored. Nixon later resigned as treasurer of the MIA and disappeared from the political scene.

Today, Nixon's contributions have been rediscovered, and he is celebrated as an unrelenting advocate, a confident negotiator, and a hardworking man who led the struggle for African American workers in Montgomery, Alabama.

MODJESKA MONTEITH SIMKINS

CIVIL RIGHTS ACTIVIST, SOUTH CAROLINA

(1899–1992)

I believe in confrontation. . . .
I believe in raising sand for those who need it.

Modjeska Monteith Simkins was an outspoken champion of the civil rights movement who fought ignorance, poverty, and racism for more than sixty years. Born on December 5, 1899, Simkins was the first of eight children born to Henry Clarence and Rachel (Hull) Monteith in Columbia, South Carolina. She was so well prepared for school that she began her education as a second-grader at Benedict College. She remained there until her college graduation in 1921.

Simkins taught medieval history at Benedict for one year and then went on to teach at Booker T. Washington High School. There she took every opportunity to make her views known. She refused to teach South Carolina history because she disliked the required textbook. She taught math until her marriage in 1929. South Carolina schools did not employ married women, so she was forced to resign.

After having three children, Simkins was ready to return to work. Her husband, who was a successful businessman, helped her get a position with the South Carolina Tuberculosis Association. During the 1930s, the years of the Great Depression, employment rates for African Americans dropped by more than one-third. The few positions available were low-skilled manual labor. Simkins and other leaders in the community met with the Works Progress Administration (WPA), a federal agency, to try to find better jobs for African Americans. As a result of their efforts, the WPA hired African American teachers and professionals for schools and special projects.

One of the first major civil rights efforts was the push for an anti-lynching bill in 1935. Simkins was one of the founders of the State Negro Citizens Committee, a group formed to pressure state legislators to support the bill. The bill was defeated, but Simkins went on to fight police brutality and discrimination as secretary of the Columbia Civic Welfare League. She also worked as the director of Negro work for the South Carolina Tuberculosis Association. She traveled throughout the state teaching proper hygiene, supervising clinics, and educating people about maternity and child-care issues.

Simkins was one of only two women on the state board of the National Association for the Advancement of Colored People (NAACP). In 1941, she was elected secretary of the Columbia chapter. That same year, she began writing for *The Lighthouse and Informer,* a publication that explored the issues and views of the state NAACP. It was the only African American publication in South Carolina. The Tuberculosis Association did not like her activism, however, and asked her to resign her position in 1942.

In 1943, Simkins became the secretary of the Teachers' Defense Fund, a committee created to raise money for NAACP-sponsored lawsuits intended to gain equal pay for African American teachers. The lawsuits succeeded, but in response, angry white politicians threatened to fire state employees who joined the NAACP. Simkins wrote the charter for a new organization, called the South Carolina Citizen's Committee, which had close ties to the NAACP.

Simkins also advocated for voting rights. She once said, "The vote is the thing that makes a difference between a free man and a slave." In 1944, the South Carolina legislature reclassified political parties as private clubs. Because private organizations had the right to discriminate, this law prevented African Americans from voting in the presidential primaries. Simkins worked with NAACP attorneys and helped to plan the successful legal strategy that changed South Carolina's voter registration laws.

In 1947, South Carolina farmer Levi Pearson asked the state to provide school buses for his children and others who had to walk as many as 8 miles (12.9 kilometers) to school. The NAACP took the lawsuit, but the white business community fought back, and Pearson could no longer borrow money or earn a living. Simkins helped to raise funds for Pearson so he could maintain his farm.

Pearson's case eventually became part of a larger lawsuit argued by NAACP attorney Thurgood Marshall. Simkins's home became the meeting place for the legal team's strategy sessions. Along with NAACP leader Rev. J. Armstrong DeLaine, Simkins wrote the declaration presenting the case, asking for equality in the schools in Clarendon County. The case became one of several that challenged the "separate but equal" doctrine and led to the U.S. Supreme Court's important decision in *Brown v. Board of Education,* ending the racial segregation of schools.

Although Simkins never belonged to the Communist Party, she was a member of groups considered to be Communist "fronts." In the 1950s, many

Members of the House Un-American Activities Committee, photographed in 1950

organizations and activists who spoke out against segregation were labeled as Communists—including the NAACP. Simkins was also friends with black leader W. E. B. Du Bois, who had been accused of being a Communist, and with leaders of the American Communist Party. Because of these friendships—and her outspoken nature and widely publicized civil rights activities—Simkins earned a place in the records of the House Un-American Activities Committee, an investigating branch of the U.S. House of Representatives.

In 1957, Simkins was replaced as secretary of the South Carolina chapter of the NAACP, but she continued to advocate for civil rights. She worked to desegregate recreation facilities in Columbia and the state mental hospital. She ran for city council twice, for the state senate, and for the school board, although she was never elected. She also continued to write letters of protest and organized local civic activities as director of the Richland County Citizen's Committee.

Fighting to the end, in 1990, a sharp, ninety-year-old Simkins delivered a passionate presentation to a group of college students, urging them to vote as a way to better their lives. Simkins's home in Columbia is more than one hundred years old, is listed on the National Register of Historic Places, and is being made into a national human rights center.

ROY WILKINS

JOURNALIST AND EXECUTIVE SECRETARY OF THE NAACP
(1901–1981)

The players in this drama of frustration and indignity are not commas or semicolons in a legislative thesis; they are people, human beings, citizens of the United States of America.

Roy Wilkins had a profound influence on the civil rights movement. He made so many contributions to his country that, on the day Wilkins died, President Ronald Reagan ordered all U.S. flags to be flown at half-mast.

Wilkins was born in St. Louis, Missouri, on August 30, 1901. He was raised by his aunt and uncle in an integrated neighborhood in St. Paul, Minnesota. As a young man, Wilkins loved to write. When he attended the University of Minnesota to major in sociology, he decided to minor in journalism.

To pay his school tuition, Wilkins took odd jobs and worked as an editor for the *Appeal,* the African American paper based in St. Paul. He also worked as night editor of the school's newspaper, the *Minnesota Daily.* When he graduated college in 1923, he took a staff writer position with the *Kansas City Call,* an African American newspaper in Missouri.

In 1931, Wilkins's work at the *Call* caught the attention of the leaders of the National Association for the Advancement of Colored People (NAACP). Wilkins left his job at the paper to work as assistant executive secretary of the NAACP, under the direction of the important civil rights leader Walter White. From that point on, Wilkins's career was dedicated to the work of the civil rights organization.

In 1932, Wilkins applied his research skills as a journalist to investigate charges of discrimination on a federally funded flood-control project in Mississippi. His findings prompted Congress to intervene in the case. Two years later, the U.S. attorney general hosted a conference on crime, but the brutal practice of lynching was not on the conference agenda. Wilkins marched in Washington, D.C., to protest and was arrested.

For fifteen years, Wilkins was the editor of the *Crisis,* the official magazine of the NAACP started by black leader and author W. E. B. Du Bois. In the 1940s, Wilkins worked as consultant to the U.S. delegation at the founding of the United Nations. By 1949, he took over as acting executive secretary of the NAACP. His title became official in 1955, and he held the position, the highest in the organization, until 1977.

Wilkins believed that African Americans could achieve equal rights through the democratic process. The strategy of the NAACP was to document significant events and to conduct their own investigations of crimes against African Americans. The organization used this information to fight for justice and to file related cases that were strong enough to change the laws.

Roy Wilkins (left) meets with President Lyndon Johnson

During the years of the civil rights movement, Wilkins often had to testify at congressional hearings, consult with presidents, and work closely with members of the NAACP and its local chapters to support the efforts of other civil rights organizations. In 1964, Wilkins received the NAACP's Spingarn Award, an award that each year honors the outstanding achievements of an African American.

In 1969, during the Vietnam War, Wilkins created the NAACP Armed Services and Veterans' Affairs Division to address the challenges and injustices faced by African American service personnel. That year, President Lyndon Johnson awarded him the Presidential Medal of Freedom, the nation's highest civilian honor. Wilkins also received the Anti-Defamation League's American Democratic Legacy Award, the Alpha Phi Psi fraternity's Outstanding Citizen Award, the American Jewish Congress's Civil Rights Award, and many others.

Wilkins retired from the NAACP in 1977. His autobiography, *Standing Fast,* was published in 1982, a year after his death. In his honor, the Roy Wilkins Center for Human Relations and Social Justice was founded at the University of Minnesota, and a sculpture memorial was constructed in his hometown of St. Paul.

ELLA JOSEPHINE BAKER

EXECUTIVE DIRECTOR OF THE SCLC AND LEADER OF THE SNCC
(1903–1986)

*The thrust is to try and develop leadership out of the group . . .
you're organizing people to be self-sufficient rather than to be
dependent upon the charismatic leader. . . .*

Ella Josephine Baker was born December 13, 1903, in Norfolk, Virginia. She grew up in a tight-knit community where everything was shared—tools, food, and often homes. Through that experience, she saw how important it was for people to stick together and solve their own problems. That idea became the central idea of her life's work. She organized communities across America to take direct action and solve their own problems. She believed that "strong people don't need strong leaders."

In the early 1900s, African Americans were not expected to have more than an elementary-school education. Baker's mother taught young Ella to read before she entered school and later sent her to Raleigh, North Carolina, to attend high school and then college. In 1927, Baker graduated from Shaw University, the first historically black college in the country to enroll women.

After graduation, Baker went to live with family members in Harlem, New York. She arrived at the height of the Harlem Renaissance, a period of great cultural activity in the African American community. She was surrounded by black music, arts, literature, and political activism. She decided to attend graduate school, but her plans were interrupted.

The stock market crash of 1929 brought the Great Depression, a period of severe economic hardship across the nation. Baker and her friend, writer George Shuyler, formed the Young Negroes Cooperative League, a branch of the federal government's Works Progress Administration (WPA). They helped blacks work together to gain economic power. During this time, she also worked as a waitress, a factory worker, and a journalist to raise money.

In 1940, Baker joined the National Association for the Advancement of Colored People (NAACP) and worked as an assistant field secretary. She traveled throughout the South, talking with people and organizing new branches of the NAACP.

Blacks in the South lived under the constant threat of violence from whites, especially if they were members of the NAACP. Baker knew that the only way to stem the tide of violence was to organize people to help themselves. She helped people in the South understand that, through the NAACP, ten members in one town could be in touch with twenty in the next town, and fifty more in the next, and so on, until they had formed a network of support across the state and the nation. She taught them that, by reaching out to each other, no one had to stand alone in the face of violence or injustice. Baker's efforts in the South created a network of support that became the basis for the civil rights movement in the decades to come.

From 1943 to 1946, Baker served as director of branches for the NAACP. The male leaders of the organization, however, were uncomfortable with her strong voice, direct manner, and powerful presence—traits they were not used to finding in most women. Baker felt that the NAACP's national leadership was too conservative, but when people asked her to make public her concerns about the leadership, she refused to criticize the organization.

Baker left her staff position but continued to volunteer at the local level. She was the first female director of the Manhattan branch, whose membership had dropped significantly. Within two years, under her direction, Baker's chapter became one of the largest branches in the country. The group led the fight to desegregate New York City public schools.

In 1956, Baker joined civil rights leaders Bayard Rustin, A. Philip Randolph, Stanley Levison, Dr. Martin Luther King Jr., Rev. Ralph Abernathy, Fred Shuttlesworth, C. K. Steele, and Coretta Scott King to discuss plans for a new organization. The next year, they founded the Southern Christian Leadership Conference (SCLC), a group committed to working together for nonviolent change. Dr. King was named its president and Ella Baker its executive director.

Baker set up the SCLC headquarters in Atlanta, Georgia. The organization wanted all Americans to understand that the mistreatment of blacks was a basic moral issue that must be addressed in order for the nation to be whole and good. They encouraged blacks to "seek justice and reject all injustice."

The SCLC trained local groups in Christian nonviolence, registered voters, opened up citizenship schools, and organized sit-ins, mass demonstrations, Freedom Rides, and antipoverty programs. Members also helped coordinate the congregations of black churches, the main organizing unit of the civil rights struggle, in nearly every community throughout the South.

For two years, Baker directed the activities of the SCLC, but she never agreed with the policy of strong central leadership. She believed the organization should empower people rather than direct them. She also felt that the SCLC was not helping women and youths to be heard.

In April 1960, Baker convinced the SCLC to sponsor a youth leaders' conference at Shaw University, her alma mater. That year, students in Greensboro, North Carolina, had organized sit-ins at segregated lunch counters as a form of protest. Their actions sparked student sit-ins across the South, which received a great deal of media attention. The SCLC wanted to gain control of the students' activities so it could direct their actions.

Baker had other plans. She set up the conference so that the students themselves had control of the agenda. Hundreds of students from across the South and the North attended. From this conference, an independent network called the Student Nonviolent Coordinating Committee (SNCC) was born.

The SNCC was the kind of organization that Baker had envisioned. Rather than follow a strong, central leader, SNCC was run by a group-centered leadership, a system in which everyone's opinions could be heard and considered. Baker resigned from the SCLC and volunteered to work as the SNCC adviser. To support herself, she took a paid job with the Young Women's Christian Association.

Many of the SNCC members were beaten and jailed, and some even lost their lives. In 1961, they faced white mob violence in protests against segregation on interstate travel on buses and trains. The SNCC was also the major force behind Freedom Summer, 1964, when hundreds of Northern college students went South to educate and register voters.

Ella Baker continued to work for civil rights in America and Africa until her death at the age of eighty-three.

MYLES HORTON

FOUNDER OF THE HIGHLANDER FOLK SCHOOL
(1905–1990)

If you believe that people are of worth, you can't treat anybody inhumanely, and that means you not only have to love and respect people, but you have to think in terms of building a society that people can profit from most, and that kind of society has to work on the principle of equality.

Myles Horton was vital to the civil rights movement of the 1950s and 1960s. His school—the Highlander Folk School in Monteagle, Tennessee— empowered millions to read, write, and vote. It also shaped the community-based, humanistic philosophies of leaders such as Septima Poinsette Clark, James Lawson, Andrew Young, Dr. Martin Luther King, and Diane Nash.

Horton was born on July 5, 1905, to hardworking parents who taught him the meaning of love and the value of education.

While attending Cumberland University in Lebanon, Tennessee, Horton quit the football team so that he would have more time to read. One summer, he directed a vacation Bible school program in Ozone, a poor community in the Tennessee mountains. Horton soon realized that the struggling people there needed more than Bible verses—they needed practical and immediate solutions. Horton organized community meetings to help people find ways to improve their living conditions.

After his experience in Ozone, Horton decided to attend what was then considered one of the more freethinking, radical schools of its kind, Union Theological Seminary in New York City. Then in 1930, he went to the University of Chicago to study sociology.

Horton decided to return to Tennessee to help the people there cope with the changes and conflicts that industry brought to their mountain communities. "I wasn't interested in resolving conflicts that would leave the same people in control and the same people powerless," he said. So he decided to start a "Southern mountain school."

Horton sought advice from Jane Addams, whose Hull House had helped thousands of immigrants in Chicago adapt to the social and economic challenges of coming to America. He also became interested in the Danish folk schools and traveled to Denmark to learn more about them. The programs in these schools taught people to work together and learn from each other and to appreciate their heritage and hopes for the future.

Horton returned to New York to raise money and finalize the plans for his school. In 1932, he and friend Don West founded the Highlander Folk School in Monteagle. A few months later, West left Highlander to start the Southern Folk School and Libraries in Kennesaw, Georgia.

By 1932, a miner's strike, which lasted for more than a year, was well under way in Tennessee. Horton got involved in the high-profile labor dispute. This experience trained the Highlander staff in the skills they needed

The Highlander Folk School in Monteagle, Tennessee

to negotiate labor disputes, work with the press, organize public-outreach efforts, and move a community to action.

When the civil rights movement began in the 1950s, the Highlander Folk School offered training and education about labor unions, workers' rights, and race relations. The school molded activists into leaders. These leaders, in turn, took what they learned at Highlander directly to the people in their communities. Rosa Parks said of her time at Highlander, "I found out for the first time in my adult life that this could be a unified society, that there was such a thing as people of differing races and backgrounds meeting together in workshops and living together in peace and harmony."

By the mid-1950s, under the direction of Septima Poinsette Clark, the Highlander Folk School began teaching illiterate African American adults how to read and write, giving them the skills they needed to vote. This program led to the formation of citizenship schools, which opened throughout the Deep South. The sudden increase in the number of African Americans who could vote and demand their rights upset many politicians and officials. They were afraid an organized black vote would jeopardize their control over the population.

During this period in American history, efforts to end segregation or organize workers were often criticized as "Communist activity." In a campaign to discredit Horton and the Highlander Folk School, Southern whites accused Horton of being part of a Communist conspiracy.

In the South, white store owners often refused to sell certain items such as razor blades, chewing gum, and beer to African Americans. Whites who attended workshops at Highlander would sometimes buy these items and share them with others at the school. In 1957, police raided the school and found these items. The Internal Revenue Service responded by refusing to let Highlander continue to operate without paying taxes. The state took control of the school's property.

With the support of leaders from around the world, Highlander fought to appeal the court's decision. In 1959, hearings were held to determine whether Highlander was part of a Communist conspiracy. The next year, the school's charter was revoked. Horton was found guilty of selling beer without a license and of violating a Tennessee state law that forbid African Americans and whites from attending school together.

In 1961, Septima Clark took the citizenship schools project to the Southern Christian Leadership Conference (SCLC). The SCLC continued much of the work in education and training that the Highlander Folk School had begun.

Horton later reopened his school and continued to prepare activists to participate in struggles for justice. The Highlander Folk School is now the Highlander Research and Education Center, located in the Great Smoky Mountains of New Market, Tennessee. The center continues to sponsor educational programs and to research community problems in order to assist social-change organizations and workers in the South and throughout the world.

THURGOOD MARSHALL

U.S. SUPREME COURT JUSTICE

(1908–1993)

In light of the sorry history of discrimination and its devastating impact on the lives of Negroes, bringing the Negro into the mainstream of American life should be a state interest of the highest order. To fail to do so is to insure that America will forever remain a divided society.

Thurgood Marshall's legal victories in the courts paved the way for all of the other social gains of the civil rights movement. His skills help end legal segregation and break the color barriers in housing, transportation, and voting rights. Thurgood Marshall brought an end to the unfair American practice of "separate but equal." His remarkable achievements are due to his fervent belief that integration of the races was absolutely necessary in order for equality of the races to ever be possible.

Marshall was born on July 2, 1908. He was named Thoroughgood after his father's grandfather, a former slave who fought for the Union army in the American Civil War. At the age of six, before entering the first grade, he asked his mother to change the name on his birth certificate to Thurgood.

The Marshall family did not have to endure the same difficult conditions that faced African Americans living in the South at that time. The Marshalls were a politically active, middle-class family in one of the rare integrated neighborhoods in Baltimore, Maryland. Norma Marshall was a kindergarten teacher in an all-black school. William Marshall was a railroad porter and a steward at an all-white club.

Thurgood's school principal had an unusual form of punishment for students who disturbed their classes. They were sent down to the basement with a copy of the U.S. Constitution and could not return to class until they had memorized a section of it. Before Marshall graduated from Frederick Douglass High School, he knew the entire Constitution by heart.

Marshall attended Lincoln University in Oxford, Pennsylvania. His mother wanted him to become a dentist, but he wanted to be a lawyer. He dreamed of attending the University of Maryland Law School, but the school only admitted whites. Segregation of the races was then the law of the land, and most of the nation's best schools were off-limits to African Americans.

Instead, Marshall attended the historically black Howard University Law School in Washington, D.C. Its new dean, Charles Hamilton Houston, was about to transform the school—which had been one of the worst law schools in the nation—into a first-rate university. Marshall's mother pawned her wedding band and engagement ring to help pay the costs for her son's education. He repaid her by becoming the top student in his class.

Houston drilled his students in constitutional law. He believed the law was the best means for protecting the rights of America's black citizens. Houston took a special interest in Marshall and allowed him and some of the other top students to work on actual cases. After graduation, Marshall faced limited job opportunities because of segregated law firms, so he opened up his own law practice.

In 1935, he took the case of Donald Gaines Murray, an African American student who had been denied admission to the University of Maryland Law School. Marshall used his deep knowledge of constitutional law to sue the school for violating the Fourteenth Amendment. He stated that the school's refusal to admit the student violated the student's right as a citizen to receive an education of the same quality as white citizens of the state. Marshall's victory was the first of many in his work for civil rights. He felt especially proud that he had been able to help a black student finally attend the very school that he himself had not been able to attend years before.

The National Association for the Advancement of Colored People (NAACP) asked Houston to review the quality of education available to African American children. Houston asked Marshall to assist him. The two men were shocked at the conditions they found. They traveled throughout the South, building a series of cases so they could challenge the U.S. Supreme Court in its ruling in *Plessy v. Ferguson*. This decision established the "separate but equal" doctrine that barred African Americans from attending the nation's best-equipped grade schools and universities.

Marshall traveled 50,000 miles (80,467 km) a year to consider and argue cases in preparation for taking on the *Plessy* verdict. In 1954, his hard work came to a head in the famous *Brown v. Board of Education* case.

In arguing the case, Marshall referred to sociological studies that showed that segregation had a negative effect on how black children felt about themselves. His brilliant approach was effective. The U.S. Supreme Court ruled that segregation in public schools was unconstitutional because it deprived African American children of an equal education, promoted self-hatred, and humiliated black students. The Court declared that segregation was against the law.

Thurgood Marshall just before taking his seat as the first black Supreme Court justice in 1967

Marshall tried a total of thirty-two cases before the U.S. Supreme Court and won twenty-nine of them. In 1967, President Lyndon Johnson appointed him to the Supreme Court. Justice Marshall worked tirelessly to protect individual rights, free speech, freedom of the press, and prisoners' rights. He retired in 1991.

Marshall's legal victories made huge strides toward establishing an integrated and equal society. He began the work, but he also realized the work was far from finished: "A child born to a black mother in a state like Mississippi—born to the dumbest, poorest sharecropper—by merely drawing its first breath in the democracy has exactly the same right as a white baby born to the wealthiest person in the United States. It's not true, but I challenge anyone to say it's not a goal worth working for."

CLARENCE MITCHELL JR.

LAWYER AND LOBBYIST

(1911–1984)

When you have a law, you have an instrument that will work for you permanently, whereas private agreements are more short-lived.

A lobbyist is a person whose job it is to influence lawmakers in creating legislation. Lobbyist Clarence Mitchell Jr. worked to persuade the president and the U.S. Congress to support reform and create laws that protected the civil rights of African Americans. His skills as a negotiator helped bring about the passage of many such laws, among them, the Civil Rights Acts of 1957, 1960, and 1964; the 1965 Voting Acts Right; and the 1968 Fair Housing Act.

Mitchell was born on March 8, 1911, in Baltimore, Maryland. He attended Lincoln University, a historically black college in Pennsylvania. After graduation, Mitchell returned home to work as a reporter for the *Baltimore Afro American*.

During the 1930s, the lynching of African Americans was still a common occurrence. Mitchell's job was to report these brutal murders. Through this experience, he began to understand the dangers of unjust laws. He saw that the best way to fight oppression and achieve equality was by changing those laws. Five years later, he ran for political office and won a seat in the Maryland House of Delegates on the Socialist Party ticket.

In 1938, Mitchell married Juanita Jackson, who was national youth director for the National Association for the Advancement of Colored People (NAACP). She was also special assistant to Walter White, executive secretary of the NAACP. Jackson later became the first African American woman to practice law in the state of Maryland.

In 1946, Clarence Mitchell became the NAACP's national labor secretary in the organization's Washington branch. His job was to develop relationships with labor unions and to lobby for civil rights legislation. Juanita Jackson Mitchell became legal counsel for the NAACP and fought segregation through the court system.

Clarence Mitchell spent so much time with members of the Senate he was sometimes referred to as the 101st senator. In 1957, Mitchell and the NAACP finally achieved passage of the first civil rights laws. The bill ensured African Americans the right to vote, but fell short of punishing those who prevented a citizen from registering. In the South, a black citizen who tried to register to vote risked loss of employment, property damage, physical harm, and even death—so the new bill was of little help.

Mitchell was disappointed that he did not get the law he wanted, but the Civil Rights Act of 1957 was the first sign of hope in eighty-two years. "The importance of getting that bill through," Mitchell said, "was that we could break the spirit of defeat around here on civil rights legislation."

President Lyndon Johnson greets African American leaders Clarence Mitchell, Martin Luther King Jr., and Ralph Abernathy.

Before the passage of the Civil Rights Act of 1960, African Americans in the South who wanted to vote had to pass a literacy test. The voting registrar might read a long section of the U.S. Constitution, for example, and ask the applicant to explain what it meant. Any applicant that could not explain to the registrar's satisfaction was not allowed to vote. Each state had its own standards for judging and refusing an applicant. The Civil Rights Act of 1960 finally prohibited anyone from interfering with another person's attempt to register or to vote—but again, the law was not easy to enforce.

Mitchell's determination and influence also helped shape the Civil Rights Act of 1964. This law required that the standards for voter registration be uniform in all the states and stated that a sixth-grade education was proof of literacy. The bill also made racial discrimination illegal in public places such as theaters, restaurants, and hotels and required employers to provide equal employment opportunities. This time, the U.S. attorney general had the power to take legal action if any state resisted the new law.

The Civil Rights Act of 1964 caused an outbreak of violence in the South, which resulted in a need for further legislation. Mitchell lobbied for the increased protection of African Americans. Congress responded with the 1965 Voting Rights Act. This bill outlawed strict literacy tests that citizens had to pass before they could register to vote, which disqualified blacks and whites who could not read. It also required that federal observers monitor voting practices in the states. The bill was considered a major victory for Mitchell, the NAACP, and for all African Americans.

In 1975, Mitchell, who had spent his career working for peace at home, was appointed a member of the United States delegation to the United Nations. In 1980, he was awarded the Presidential Medal of Freedom.

Two days after Mitchell's death on March 18, 1984, this tribute appeared in an editorial in the *Washington Post:* "In the halls of Congress he won victories without making enemies because he was strong without ever being mean. Beginning with the Civil Rights Act of 1957, every antidiscrimination statute for a quarter of a century bears his mark. His life's work, inspiring those who shared his hopes and eventually persuading almost all of those who hesitated, profoundly changed and uplifted the nation."

AMZIE MOORE

CIVIL RIGHTS ACTIVIST, MISSISSIPPI
(1911–1982)

He's either very brave or very stupid. Amzie Moore moved through Mississippi a free man, with no fear at the height of its most violent period in history. His tireless advocacy and courage, improved the quality of life for Mississippians across the Delta.
—*Bayard Rustin*

African Americans in Mississippi started their own freedom movement long before the civil rights movement of the 1950s and 1960s—and Amzie Moore was there. Moore, who registered to vote in 1936, helped to start the first Negro Boy Scout troop in Cleveland, Mississippi. In 1940, he and several thousand other African Americans attended a rally at the Cotton Makers Jubilee at Delta State University in Cleveland, hoping to improve schools and modernize life in the Mississippi Delta. These types of grassroots activities were a way of life for Moore.

Amzie Moore was born September 23, 1911, on the Wilkin plantation near the Grenada and Carroll county lines. At age fifteen, he moved to Cleveland, where he worked for the U.S. Postal Service. When World War II began in 1942, Moore was drafted into the army, where he served as a fighter pilot and taught airplane recognition.

During his tour of duty, Moore traveled throughout the world. In Burma, he was once ordered to tell African American soldiers that conditions in the United States would be better for them when they returned. In 1946, Moore returned to Cleveland, his job at the post office, and the new war at home. In Mississippi, African Americans were being killed every week. The NAACP, which Moore had joined during his tour of duty, linked the murders with a fanatic group of Civil War veterans called the Home Guard.

With a loan from Standard Life Insurance Company, Moore bought a piece of land on Highway 61 and built a combination gas station, beauty shop, grocery, and restaurant. Moore's gas station provided the only restrooms for African American drivers between Memphis and Vicksburg. This strip of businesses became the headquarters for the area's civil rights efforts.

By 1950, Moore and T. R. M. Howard, a well-known surgeon, cofounded the Regional Council of Negro Leadership (RCNL). Moore served as vice chairman of the RCNL, which had one hundred thousand members from at least half the counties in Mississippi. The first general meeting of the RCNL attracted several thousand people and featured prominent speakers, such as Charles Diggs, Thurgood Marshall, and Congressman William Dawson. The RCNL sought to meet the practical needs of its supporters. It taught residents about the U.S. Constitution and held regular meetings so people could share information and discuss the challenges they faced when trying to register and vote.

The RCNL built a network of ministers, businesspeople, and fraternal groups in the South and the Northeast. The word was out about the difficulties faced by African Americans in Mississippi, and leaders like Bayard Rustin visited to get a firsthand look. News stories ran in African American magazines and newspapers, prompting people to send money. A group called In Friendship sent clothes, sewing machines, and other supplies to needy families of the Mississippi Delta. The group had been founded by Rustin and fellow activists Ella Baker and Stanley Levison to provide aid to the victims of racial terrorism in the South.

In 1955, Moore was elected president of the Cleveland chapter of the NAACP. He teamed up with Medgar Evers, the NAACP field director in Jackson. Together, they increased the NAACP's membership in the area to more than four hundred. Moore also collaborated with the national office leader, Roy Wilkins, to set up conferences and fund-raisers. He eventually became vice president of the state conference of NAACP branches.

Moore had no interest in boycotts and sit-ins. He knew that if African Americans could register and vote, they would have the power to elect their own people into political office and to make real changes in their communities. In the state of Mississippi, less than 5 percent of the predominantly African American population was registered to vote. The threat of violence from white segregationists was so great that there were counties without any African Americans on the lists of voters. Moore worked with Herman Perry to start the Bolivar County Voter's League in his own district, which was two-thirds black.

White segregationists began to organize in the mid-1950s, too. The White Citizens' Council (WCC) was established in 1955. The WCC were respected businessmen whose mission was very similar to that of the Ku Klux Klan: to force a half million African Americans to leave the South. In their first year, the WCC's membership was about twenty-five thousand. In year two, their numbers grew to eighty thousand. In response to this dramatic increase, Moore sent a representative, Sam Block, to Greenwood, where the WCC's headquarters was located, to educate and organize the African Americans living in the area.

Moore built strong relationships with people throughout the state of Mississippi. He located witnesses to testify at the Emmett Till murder trial. He also introduced activists from other parts of the country to local communities and leaders in the Delta. His residence operated as a "safe house" for local civil rights recruits and for activists from across the country. He hosted Bayard Rustin, Ella Baker, Thurgood Marshall, Lawrence Guyot, Robert Moses, and many other prominent leaders of the civil rights movement.

African Americans who worked for whites often lost their jobs after voting or after attempting to register to vote. As director of Operation Freedom, Moore ensured that those who lost their jobs would have enough money to survive.

Whenever he could, Moore lobbied for funds and special programs for Bolivar County. He also organized the first Head Start program in the county, which helped 1,400 white and 7,600 African American families. The program had a budget of one million dollars, but Moore did not draw a salary.

When Moore retired from the postal service, he took a position as manager of the National Council of Negro Women's Turnkey Project, which provided low-income housing for families in need. Moore was responsible for the construction of a large housing development in the East Gate area of Cleveland. Moore Avenue in East Gate is named in his honor.

In 2001, the city of Cleveland officially rededicated Shady Grove Park and renamed it Amzie Moore Park. The park features a granite monument listing Moore's many contributions to the civil rights movements.

ISAIAH DEQUINCEY NEWMAN

CIVIL RIGHTS ACTIVIST, SOUTH CAROLINA
(1911–1985)

*I kept that in my heart for a long time and I held it against my father.
There was a man being burned alive, and my father wouldn't turn a
hand to help him. Of course, I learned since then had he gone to give
help, he would have been shot down, just killed.*

The Reverend Isaiah DeQuincey Newman was
born on April 17, 1911, in Darlington County,
South Carolina. One incident from his childhood
left a lasting impression. The family lived near a camp
that housed prisoners. Newman remembered that one
night, the Ku Klux Klan, a white supremacist group,
set fire to the lockup where a black prisoner was held.
The man's screams for help woke Newman. He pleaded
with his father to go and help the man, but his father
just told him to go back to bed. Only many years later
did Newman understand that his father could not have
helped without losing his own life.

"I. D.," as he was called by his friends, attended
public schools in Williamsburg County. While he was

still a young man, he decided that he wanted to get a college education and become a preacher. To earn money, he worked on street corners and in shops shining shoes. Newman attended Claflin College, a historically African American college in Orangeburg, South Carolina. In 1933, he graduated from Clark College in Atlanta, Georgia, and then earned his divinity degree from Gammon Theological Seminary.

As a newly ordained minister, Newman took a position as student pastor in a small church of sharecroppers in Red Oak, Georgia. The sharecropping life was hard, and the abuse of plantation owners kept the workers in poverty and debt. When one sharecropper became ill, Newman visited the plantation owner and urged him to put the sick worker in the hospital. The angry owner cocked his shotgun and aimed it at Newman, demanding that he leave and never come back.

Newman was committed to finding a way to improve conditions for African Americans. He returned to South Carolina with a new wife and a new mission. In 1943, he was a key organizer of the Orangeburg branch of the National Association for the Advancement of Colored People (NAACP). Having learned the dangers of direct confrontation firsthand, he chose to negotiate for change instead. Newman waged his fight for freedom through his work with the NAACP and held several leadership positions at the state level.

By 1956, the political climate in South Carolina was harsh. The 1954 *Brown v. Board of Education* decision had forced integration in the schools and opened the door for an end to segregation in public places. Rather than integrate its state parks and schools, however, the state of South Carolina chose to close them entirely. State employees could be fired simply for being a member of the NAACP. One newspaper described the 1956 South Carolina legislative session as the "segregationist session."

In 1960, Newman was appointed field director for the state branch of the NAACP. He led the group through some of its most bitter and violent periods. As field director, he was responsible for developing ways to challenge the state institutions that imposed segregation. Newman's calm leadership style was both admired and challenged. He forced change, but he did so in a manner that minimized the violence that accompanied change in so many other states. Journalist Jack Bass said, "He knew when to push and how far to push."

In 1961, Newman decided to push a little harder. He staged a "wade-in" protest at Myrtle Beach State Park, which was usually closed to African Americans. He was arrested by the local police and escorted to the county line. After his release, a mob of angry whites chased him in cars from one end of the county to the other at speeds up to 120 miles (193 km) per hour, but he escaped them.

The NAACP and other civil rights groups persisted in their efforts, and the sit-ins, demonstrations, and boycotts continued. In 1966, Newman led a demonstration outside the office of Senator Edgar Brown, and the senator had to be physically restrained from attacking the protesters.

The brutal Orangeburg Massacre of 1968, in which three African American students were killed and others injured, is part of the story of South Carolina's civil rights struggle. Violence in the state was minimal, however, compared to hot spots like Mississippi and Alabama. Many attributed the relatively peaceful change in South Carolina to the leadership of Newman and others.

In 1969, Newman retired from the NAACP and returned to preaching and other state and civic activities. From 1970 to 1974, he served as founding president of the Statewide Homes Foundation. He later worked as an organizer and director of the Office of Rural Development and as a commissioner of the South Carolina Housing Authority.

Newman was a delegate to the Democratic National Conventions of 1968, 1972, and 1980. In 1983, he became South Carolina's first African American senator since 1887. To recognize Newman's many contributions, the state created a special professorship in his honor at the University of South Carolina—the school's first endowed chair named for an African American.

BAYARD TAYLOR RUSTIN

COFOUNDER OF THE **SCLC**

(1912–1987)

Unjust social laws and patterns do not change because supreme courts deliver just decisions. . . . Social progress comes from struggle; all freedom demands a price. . . . If anyone at this date in history believes that [racism] can be settled without violence, he is mistaken and fails to realize the ends to which men can be driven to hold on to what they consider their privileges. . . . This is why [participants] must pledge themselves to nonviolence in word and deed. For in this way alone can the inevitable violence be reduced to a minimum.

Bayard Rustin brought the nonviolent protest tactics of the Indian leader Mohandas Gandhi to the American civil rights movement. He helped promote Dr. Martin Luther King Jr. as an international symbol for peace and justice. Through his powerful determination and forceful drive, he helped win some of the greatest victories of the civil rights movement.

Bayard Taylor Rustin was born on March 17, 1912, in West Chester, Pennsylvania. He was raised by his grandparents, Julia and Janifer Rustin. Julia taught young Bayard the principles of her Quaker faith: that all people are created equal before God; it's important to treat everyone with love and respect; and violence is never the way to solve a problem.

Julia Rustin was not only a Quaker, she was also a member of the National Association for the Advancement of Colored People (NAACP). Some of the organization's highest-ranking leaders, such as W. E. B. Du Bois and James Weldon Johnson, stayed with the Rustin family when they toured the country on business.

Bayard Rustin attended Wilberforce University in Ohio, the oldest private university for African Americans in the country. In 1936, he left without taking his final exams. Later that year, he joined the Communist Party.

In 1937, Rustin left Pennsylvania for Harlem, New York, and enrolled at City College. He became an organizer in the Young Communists League. At that time, the Communists were opposed to racial injustice, and he fought with them against segregation and American involvement in World War II. When the United States entered the war in 1941, however, the party supported segregation in the armed forces, so Rustin broke away from the group.

That year, Rustin met two men who would be great influences in his life— A. J. Muste of Fellowship of Reconciliation (FOR) and A. Philip Randolph, the president of the Brotherhood of Sleeping Car Porters and one of the most influential black men in America.

Muste was impressed by Rustin's organizational skills and appointed him as FOR's race relations secretary. FOR had championed nonviolence as a means of social change since 1914. Rustin traveled throughout the country, working to foster communication and understanding between racial groups.

In 1941, A. Philip Randolph pressured President Franklin Roosevelt to end discrimination against blacks in war industry jobs. Randolph threatened to lead a protest march to Washington, D.C., and Rustin eagerly helped organize the youth division of the planned march. When Roosevelt gave in and signed an executive order for fair hiring practices, Randolph called off the march. Rustin, however, felt cheated out of a chance to take direct action and push the nation further toward racial equality. He broke off his relationship with Randolph.

Rustin helped two other members of FOR, James Farmer and George Houser, to form the Congress of Racial Equality (CORE). They studied Mohandas Gandhi's methods of nonviolent resistance, which were successful in bringing change to India in its struggle with the oppressive rule of England.

Because Rustin was a member of the pacifist Quaker church, he did not have to serve in the armed forces. The government considered the Quaker church a "peace church" and provided an alternative type of service for its members. But Rustin had seen many men who did not belong to a peace church receive harsh prison sentences for refusing to join the war effort. Because of that, he refused to take the easy way out and instead accepted a prison sentence. He was charged with violating the Selective Service Act, which requires American citizens to serve in the military if called, and spent three years in Lewisburg Penitentiary.

While in prison, Rustin organized protests against segregated seating in the dining hall. He told the prison warden, "Segregation is to me a basic injustice. Since I believe it to be so, I must attempt to remove it. . . . To accept it is to perpetuate it."

When Rustin was released in 1947, he met with leaders of FOR, CORE, and the NAACP to organize the first bus ride protest against segregation. Later, these protests became known as Freedom Rides. In 1946, the U.S. Supreme Court ruled that segregation in interstate travel was unconstitutional, but Southern states still had Jim Crow laws that enforced segregation. Rustin intended to enforce the Court's decision.

Thurgood Marshall, the head of the legal department for the NAACP, warned Rustin that his plans would "result in wholesale slaughter with no good achieved," but Rustin was determined to see it through. On April 9, 1947, Rustin, eight other blacks, and nine whites traveled on buses and trains throughout the South. The blacks sat in the front seats, usually reserved for white, and the whites took the back seats, which were set aside for blacks. They called this first ride to end segregation the Journey of Reconciliation.

Rustin and the others were repeatedly arrested, fined, and jailed for not sitting in the segregated sections. Each time, the NAACP sent lawyers to help them, but in North Carolina, Rustin and several others were sentenced to thirty days of hard labor on a chain gang.

Members of CORE continued their bus protests, and the experience became invaluable during the civil rights actions of the 1950s and 1960s. In 1955, when Rosa Parks refused to give up her seat on the bus to a white man, Dr. Martin Luther King asked Rustin to help organize the Montgomery Bus Boycott.

Energized by the successful bus boycott, King, Rustin, and others formed the Southern Christian Leadership Conference (SCLC). Rustin, who believed that nonviolence was the key to victory in the civil rights movement, became one of King's main advisers. The SCLC made a commitment to oppose racial injustice only through nonviolent social protest, maintaining that "not one hair on the head of a white person should be harmed" in the fight for civil rights.

In 1963, Rustin organized a March on Washington. On August 28, between 250,000 and 400,000 people of all races attended the daylong peaceful demonstration. The event convinced President John F. Kennedy and members of Congress that the nation was ready and waiting for them to pass the Civil Rights Act, which was signed into law the next year, outlawing segregation and discrimination.

Rustin once said that his social activism was not due to his race. "Rather it is rooted fundamentally in my Quaker upbringing. . . . Those values were based on the concept of a single human family and the belief that all members of the family are equal."

DAISY BATES

FRIEND AND ADVISER TO THE LITTLE ROCK NINE
(1914–1999)

The *Brown v. Board of Education* ruling of 1954 was a bittersweet victory for the civil rights movement. The U.S. Supreme Court had ruled that segregation in the schools was against the law—but most Southern states did not act quickly to support the ruling. Only Texas and Arkansas began to desegregate their schools that year. Many people felt threatened and resisted the change. The habits and customs they had lived with for many years had deep roots.

The town of Little Rock, Arkansas, announced it would integrate its schools over the course of several years. The school board claimed it needed more time because it feared the danger and difficulty of sudden change.

Daisy Lee Gatson Bates, who was president of the state branch of the National

Association for the Advancement of Colored People (NAACP), led the fight for the immediate integration of the schools. She and her husband published the *Arkansas State Press*, a newspaper for the African American community. Accompanied by photographers from her newspaper, Bates took African American children to enroll in white schools and documented the school's refusal to admit those students. Pressured by the constant media attention, the Little Rock Board of Education agreed to integrate Little Rock Central High School in 1957.

Bates handpicked nine African American students to be the first to attend Central High. She chose students she believed had the strength to succeed academically and also to withstand the harsh treatment they might face. These students—Jefferson Thomas, Carlotta Walls, Gloria Ray, Elizabeth Eckford, Thelma Mothershed, Melba Pattillo, Terrance Roberts, Minniejean Brown, and Ernest Green—came to be known as the Little Rock Nine. Bates encouraged the students and gave them guidance on how to behave in a hostile environment. She instructed them to always remain proud and calm and to never respond to mistreatment with anger or violence.

A group of white mothers in Little Rock, who called themselves the Mother's League, opposed the integration of the school. Encouraged by Arkansas governor Orval Faubus, the women appeared in court, claiming that their children were arming themselves in preparation for a fight. They appeared in the county court asking that the black students be barred from Central High. The court granted their request and delayed the integration indefinitely—but NAACP attorneys Thurgood Marshall and Wiley Branton challenged the ruling in a U.S. district court and won.

Faubus still claimed that violence would break out at the school when the new students arrived. He arranged for 250 members of the state's National Guard to surround the school as a form of protection. The school board then released a statement asking the black students to remain home until the "dilemma is legally resolved." No one but the National Guardsmen showed up on the first day of school. The federal judge, Ronald Davies, again ordered the school board to proceed with the integration immediately.

On September 4, the Little Rock Nine planned to meet at the corner of 12th Street and Park Avenue at 8:30 A.M. One of the students, Elizabeth Eckford, did not receive the phone message, so that morning she set out for Central High alone. As she approached the school, she ignored the name-calling and threats because she believed the National Guard was there to protect her. When she tried to enter the school, however, a guard raised his bayonet to block her. A wild group of parents and children demanded a lynching. Bates and her husband heard a radio news report of what was happening at the school and raced to Eckford's rescue. Before they arrived, a white woman named Grace Lorch had led the young girl away from the mob and took her home.

On September 23, the Little Rock Nine gathered at the Bates home to prepare again to integrate Central High. African American reporters arrived at the school before the nine students and were mistaken for their parents. One reporter was hit in the head with a brick and brutalized by the angry mob. The court had ordered the governor to remove the National Guard, and the police that were there looked on and did nothing.

The Little Rock Nine arrived at the school with a police escort and entered through the side door as white segregationists looked on, cursed, and wept. Mob anger grew, and one officer suggested the nine children draw straws to decide which one should be lynched to appease the crowd. The police chief then stepped in and quickly loaded all nine students into two cars and made a high-speed escape through the crowd.

President Dwight D. Eisenhower decided to send the Arkansas National Guard and the U.S. 101st Airborne Division to Central High to protect the Little Rock Nine. This action marked the first time a U.S. president had

Daisy Bates and the Little Rock Nine

asked U.S. troops to subdue the country's own citizens. A crowd of angry segregationists confronted the guards. A dozen guards raised their bayonets, showing the mob they intended to follow the president's orders, and the crowd dispersed.

The army patrol remained at the school through November. Even then, the nine students worried which part of the hall would be safest, and what sort of things might be thrown at them that day. Melba Pattillo recalled praying for the courage to climb the stairs to her homeroom. The administration had placed each of the nine African American students in a different homeroom and in different classes throughout the day. The Little Rock Nine—the only black students in a school of 2,500 whites—were not able to help each other or stick together for support.

Bates stood by the students all year. The Little Rock Nine met at her house every morning before school and often in the afternoon after school. Bates also asked other NAACP leaders, experts in nonviolent protest, to teach the students how to respond to violence and aggression.

Bates and her husband were harassed, too. Their home was set on fire several times. Angry townspeople threw sticks of dynamite at the house and burned Ku Klux Klan crosses on the front yard. They could no longer afford to publish their newspaper because white businesses stopped buying advertisements.

At the start of the next school year, Governor Faubus closed all the public high schools in Little Rock. Most of the white students went to private schools, but many other students—including the Little Rock Nine—did not attend school that year. In 1959, the U.S. Supreme Court ruled that the school closings were unconstitutional. By August of that year, the schools were reopened, and black and white students attended classes that fall.

The Little Rock Nine eventually went on to college—and some to graduate school—to study journalism, psychology, accounting, science, finance, and education. In 1987, Little Rock opened the Daisy Bates Elementary School. In 1988, Bates won the National Book Award for *The Long Shadow of Little Rock,* her personal account of her experiences.

In 1999, President Bill Clinton awarded Daisy Bates and the Little Rock Nine the Congressional Gold Medal of Honor for their heroic contribution to the civil rights movement. In his speech, the president said, "They persevered, they endured, and they prevailed, but it was at a great cost to themselves. . . . Like so many Americans, I can never fully repay my debt to these nine people, because, with their innocence, they purchased more freedom for me, too, and for all white people."

FANNIE LOU HAMER

CIVIL RIGHTS ACTIVIST AND COFOUNDER OF THE MFDP

(1917–1977)

What was the point of being scared? The only thing they could do to me was kill me and it seemed like they'd been trying to do that a little bit at a time ever since I could remember.

Fannie Lou Hamer was born on October 6, 1917, in the hills of Sunflower County, Mississippi. Her parents were sharecroppers, and she was the youngest of twenty children. Life was difficult for the large family. "We never hardly had enough to eat; we didn't have clothes to wear," she remembered. "We had to work real hard."

Sharecropping was a farming system established after slavery. Workers were allowed to live on a plantation in return for working the land. When the crop was harvested, the owner was supposed to split the profits in half with the sharecropper. Plantation owners often abused the system, however. They would charge the sharecroppers for fertilizer and other expenses, leaving the farmer with little profit or, in many cases, a large debt to the plantation owner.

Fannie began working on the plantation at age six, and she often had to miss school to pick cotton or to cut and burn stalks. After she married Perry "Pap" Hamer, she and her husband moved to the town of Ruleville, Mississippi, where they worked together as sharecroppers and ran a small saloon.

The Hamers and other families in the Mississippi Delta region had little education and not much time to do anything except work the fields. They knew little about issues like voting and constitutional rights. One evening in 1962, Fannie attended a meeting at the local church. The guest speaker was Rev. James Bevel, a civil rights organizer, who spoke about the right to vote. He asked for volunteers who would be willing to resist the harsh Jim Crow laws that kept African Americans in the South from exercising that right. Hamer was the first to raise her hand.

At first, Hamer could not register because she did not pass the literacy test. When the landowner heard that she was trying to vote, he forced her to leave the plantation where she had lived and worked for eighteen years. She stayed with a cousin and then at the home of a family friend—where she was harassed and shot at sixteen times.

In December 1962, Hamer passed the literacy test. A Jim Crow law, however, also required her to prove she had already paid two years of poll taxes—the fee required to vote. Of course, because Hamer was a first-time voter, she had never paid any poll taxes, so she was not allowed to vote.

Hamer became a field secretary for the Student Nonviolent Coordinating Committee (SNCC) and was active in the organization's voter registration drives. She went door-to-door teaching black people about their right to vote and be heard. In June 1963, police arrested Hamer and a group of civil rights workers in Winona, Mississippi, because "their bus was the wrong color." Hamer and another activist, Annie Ponder, were taken to a county jail and brutally beaten by prison inmates—on direct order of the sheriff. SNCC lawyers got the two women out of jail and filed suit against the Winona police, who were found not guilty.

Despite the dangers and frustrations, Hamer continued her work for civil rights. Now that she knew she had a choice, she couldn't do anything else. "I do remember, one time, a man came to me after the students began to work in Mississippi, and he said the white people were getting tired and they were getting tense and anything might happen. Well, I asked him, how long he thinks we had been getting tired? . . . All my life I've been sick and tired. Now I'm sick and tired of being sick and tired."

Later, Hamer worked with the Freedom Schools to teach African Americans about the U.S. Constitution and to explain how to fill out voter registration forms. She spoke out for the 850,000 unregistered African American voters of Mississippi when she ran for Congress against Representative Jamie Whitten. Although she lost the election, Hamer was able to finally cast her first vote—and she voted for herself.

When Hamer and eight others tried to attend a meeting of the all-white Mississippi Democratic Party, they found that the door was locked. The small group sat on the steps of the building and organized their own group. They elected a chairman, secretary, and delegates. On April 24, 1964, at the Masonic Temple in Jackson, the Mississippi Freedom Democratic Party (MFDP) was founded.

In August, Hamer and several other delegates of the MFDP went to the Democratic National Convention in Atlantic City. They planned to challenge the seating of the all-white delegation from Mississippi, which did not accurately represent the population of the state. The MFDP was offered only two seats. "We didn't come all this way for no two seats," Hamer said.

Hamer addressed the convention, and her speech was broadcast on national television. She shared the story of the cruel beating she received in that Mississippi jail and spoke about the murders, violence, and abuses African American faced when trying to exercise their Constitutional right to vote. President Lyndon Johnson did not allow the entire speech to air, and he quickly interrupted with his own presentation, but Hamer had shined a spotlight on issues that could no longer be ignored. One year later, Congress passed the Voting Rights Act, which lifted all restrictions on people's right to vote.

Hamer believed that white Americans could not be free until African Americans were free. "As I liberate myself, I liberate him." She began to work with poor people—black and white—to end the extreme poverty in the Mississippi Delta. In 1969, she founded Freedom Farms, a co-op of more than 700 acres on which people could grow their own vegetables. Freedom Farms fed more than five thousand families.

In 1972, when the civil rights movement began to focus on the rights of women, Hamer helped to found the National Women's Political Caucus. After Hamer's death in 1977, Andrew Young, former U.S. ambassador to the United Nations and mayor of Atlanta, described her as "the woman who shook the foundation of this nation."

JAMES LEONARD FARMER JR.

CIVIL RIGHTS LEADER, COFOUNDER OF CORE

(1920–1999)

The fight for freedom is combined with the fight for equality, and we must realize that this is the fight for America—not just black America but all America.

James Farmer Jr. was born in Marshall, Texas, on January 12, 1920. His father was the son of a slave who became a Methodist minister and a college professor. James Farmer Sr. taught literature in Greek, Aramaic, and Hebrew and is believed to be the first African American from the state of Texas to earn a doctoral degree. Farmer's mother, Pearl Marion Houston, was a teacher.

Young James was a brilliant student and entered Wiley College when he was fourteen years old. In 1938, he entered Howard University to study religion. He learned about Mohandas Gandhi, who led successful nonviolent protests in India. Gandhi was a pacifist, a person who does not believe in war or violence as a way to solve problems. Farmer adopted Gandhi's philosophy.

After graduation, Farmer decided not to become a minister. Churches in the South were segregated, so black and white congregations could not sit together to worship. "I didn't see how I could honestly preach the Gospel of Christ in a church that practiced discrimination," Farmer said.

When the United States entered World War II in 1941, Farmer refused to enter military service. The government allowed people who had strong religious beliefs against war to register as "conscientious objectors." Farmer went to work for a pacifist organization, Fellowship of Reconciliation (FOR), as their race relations secretary.

In 1942, Farmer and a white friend, George Houser, stopped for coffee and doughnuts at Jack Spratt's Coffee Shop in Chicago, Illinois. The counter man made them wait and tried to charge each of them a dollar for doughnuts that cost only a nickel. When Farmer and Houser objected, the man threw their money on the floor and ordered them to leave the store.

Farmer, Houser, Bayard Rustin, and a group of others decided it was time to take direct action against segregation in America. They formed the Congress of Racial Equality (CORE). CORE was an interracial organization made up mostly of students committed to nonviolent protests and demonstrations. Farmer organized the nation's first sit-in protest at the Jack Spratt Coffee Shop—and the action succeeded in changing the restaurant's policy.

CORE grew into a nationwide organization that had a powerful impact on the civil rights movement. In just a few years, it had more than seventy chapters and more than sixty thousand members throughout the country. CORE workers trained local communities and groups to conduct nonviolent demonstrations and helped thousands of African Americans stand up for their rights as American citizens.

James Farmer in his New York office in 1964

Farmer and Rustin organized CORE's first Freedom Ride—a nonviolent protest by bus. In 1944, Irene Morgan had started out on a bus trip from the North, which did not have segregated seating. When her bus passed into the Southern states, she was arrested for violating the segregation laws of the South.

In 1946, the U.S. Supreme Court ruled it was unreasonable to stop buses and trains that traveled between states in order to separate the black and white passengers as they traveled through the South. In 1947, Farmer and Rustin decided to see whether or not the Court's decision was being enforced. They organized a Freedom Ride that they called the Journey of Reconciliation.

Nine whites and blacks, all trained in nonviolent action, planned to board interstate buses in the upper South. The whites were to sit in the section for blacks and the blacks in the section for whites. When asked to move, the nine passengers would refuse, referring to the U.S. Supreme Court's decision in *Morgan v. The Commonwealth of Virginia*.

The riders met with heavy resistance. They were beaten, fined, and jailed. In North Carolina, a judge turned his back on their defense attorney and then sentenced Rustin and several others to thirty days of hard labor on a chain gang.

Many people were unwilling to resist what had long been the way of life in the South—but Farmer was determined. He went from community to community, and organized blacks and whites to fight peacefully against discrimination.

In 1961, Farmer was elected the national director of CORE. He and other CORE leaders decided to stage more Freedom Rides. This time, they planned to travel by bus all the way to New Orleans, Louisiana. The violence began when they reached the Deep South.

The riders were attacked by a mob at the bus station in Anniston, Alabama. The tires were slashed, but the bus driver drove away on flat tires to save their lives. The bus was then firebombed, and the riders barely escaped before it was engulfed in flames. The violence continued through Birmingham and Montgomery, Alabama. The bus companies refused to carry the Freedom Riders any farther for fear of losing more buses, and drivers were not willing to risk their lives. The threat of more violence forced the riders to fly to New Orleans.

A determined group of students from Nashville, Tennessee—members of the Student Nonviolent Coordinating Committee (SNCC)—traveled to Montgomery to continue the Freedom Ride. Dr. Martin Luther King Jr. also went there to lend his support. The government sent in U.S. marshals to guard the students as they rode out of Montgomery. When they arrived in Jackson, Mississippi, the Freedom Riders were arrested for "disturbing the peace." Farmer spent forty days in jail, and the Freedom Riders never made it to New Orleans.

That summer, students from all over the North flocked to the South. Many were arrested, and the news media followed the developments closely.

Much of the country was shocked by what they saw on television and read in the newspapers. The citizens' outrage finally forced the government to enforce the U.S. Supreme Court decision. Six months after the Freedom Rides, the government ordered the integration of all interstate buses and terminal facilities.

Farmer continued his civil rights work with CORE, turning his attention to illiteracy and unemployment among African Americans. He taught courses at Lincoln University in Pennsylvania and at Mary Washington College in Virginia, stressing the lessons that history can teach new generations.

In 1998, Farmer was awarded the Congressional Medal of Freedom, the highest honor in the land. He once told a reporter, the fight against racism in the 1960s "required tough skulls and guts . . . now it requires intellect, training and education." He realized that the battle for equality was not yet over, but he also recognized that the methods for achieving victory had changed.

DR. JOSEPH LOWERY

CIVIL RIGHTS ACTIVIST, ALABAMA

(1921–)

We've been an umbrella in the forty years of rain. We saw a fire burning in the souls of Black America. Water hoses couldn't wash it out, billy clubs couldn't beat it out and jails couldn't lock it out.

Joseph Lowery, the man who has become known as the Dean of the Civil Rights Movement, was born in Huntsville, Alabama, on October 6, 1921. After he finished high school in Huntsville, Lowery attended Knoxville College, Payne College and Theological Seminary, and the Chicago Ecumenical Institute, where he later earned a doctorate of divinity degree.

Lowery's first job during the civil rights movement was to head the Alabama Civic Affairs Association, a prominent local organization committed to desegregating the buses and public places of Mobile, Alabama. Powerful white segregationists

Civil rights activists march from Selma to Montgomery in 1985 to commemorate the twentieth anniversary of the historic 1965 march.

opposed the association, and in the mid-1950s, the state sued Lowery and four other ministers and won three million dollars. The U.S. Supreme Court later reversed the decision, and Lowery's property, which had been seized after the initial ruling, was returned.

In 1957, Lowery worked alongside Dr. Martin Luther King Jr. to form the Southern Christian Leadership Conference (SCLC). He also served as the group's first vice president. In 1965, Lowery was named chairman of the delegation of protesters in the famous march from Selma to Montgomery. His job was to present the group's list of demands to Governor George Wallace, who was known for his fierce opposition to integration.

Lowery marched alongside his fellow ministers Dr. King, Ralph Abernathy, and Fred Shuttlesworth, as well as many others throughout the 1960s. In the 1970s, Lowery cofounded the Black Leadership Forum, which worked to destroy the South African system of apartheid.

In 1990, Lowery led a workshop on human relations for former members of the Ku Klux Klan who had attacked a civil rights march in Decatur, Alabama, years earlier. A federal judge had ordered the Klan members to take the workshop as part of the settlement of a lawsuit against the white supremacist group. Several of the Klan members were also sentenced to jail.

Lowery spent forty years in service to the SCLC, serving ten years as executive vice president and another ten years as the first board chairman. In 1977, he was appointed national president, a position he held for twenty years.

In 1997, twenty-nine years after the assassination of Dr. King, Lowery demanded that James Earl Ray, the convicted killer, be retried. He did not believe that Ray had the intellect or the resources to act alone in the shooting. "I think the American people are entitled to know all of those who were possibly involved in the assassination of Martin Luther King Jr. along with whatever role James Earl Ray played," Lowery said. "The forces that killed King are still operative in this country . . . racial hate, greed, terrorism. And until we know as much about them as possible, there'll be no healing."

Lowery retired from the ministry in 1997 and from the SCLC in 1998— but he did not stop working for American civil rights. Hoping to reach the hip-hop generation, he recorded a song with rap artist Nate the Great, encouraging young people to vote. He has also led peacekeeping delegations to the Middle East and Central America.

"We all felt called by God to participate in a divine journey from wrong to right, from injustice to justice. . . . It's been a great journey and I'm just glad that God picked me," Lowery once said.

CONSTANCE BAKER MOTLEY

Attorney, Politician, Federal Judge
(1921–2005)

*Something which we think is impossible now
is not impossible in another decade.*

Constance Baker Motley was born on September 14, 1921, in New Haven, Connecticut. She was the ninth of twelve children of West Indian immigrants from the Caribbean island of Nevis. Her mother, Rachel Baker, was founder of the local chapter of the National Association for the Advancement of Colored People (NAACP). Her father, Willoughby Baker, was a chef at Yale University. The community of New Haven had very few African Americans at that time, so Motley was often the only student of color in her classes.

Motley was an excellent student, but with twelve children, her parents could not afford to send them all to college. After high school, she took a job as a domestic worker. Later, she worked for the National Youth Administration, a federal program that provided students with part-time jobs. Motley was an eloquent speaker. After a speech she gave at the local community center, Clarence Blakelee, a wealthy white businessman, was so impressed by her that he offered to pay for her college education.

Motley was curious about life in the South, so she enrolled at the historically black Fisk University in Nashville, Tennessee. In 1942, she transferred to New York University, where she completed a degree in economics. The following year, she was accepted to the prestigious Columbia University School of Law. When Motley informed her employer that she had been accepted to the school, he said, "That's the dumbest thing I ever heard, a complete waste of time. Women don't get anywhere in the law."

While at Columbia, Motley met Thurgood Marshall, who hired her to work as a law clerk in the New York office of the NAACP Legal Defense and Educational Fund. In 1948, Motley passed the bar exam and became a lawyer—a profession that had few African American women at that time. "I was on the ground floor of the civil rights movement without even knowing it," she said.

Marshall soon promoted Motley to the position of assistant legal counsel for the defense fund. She prepared the briefs for the landmark *Brown v. Board of Education* lawsuit in 1954. Some of her early cases helped support the Little Rock Nine's admission to Central High School in Little Rock, Arkansas, and James Meredith's admission to the University of Mississippi. Motley successfully argued for the reinstatement of one thousand African American youth who were expelled from Birmingham schools because they had participated in a protest demonstration. She was the first woman to argue a case before the U.S. Supreme Court, and she won nine of the ten cases she presented before the Court between 1961 and 1964. She also served as legal counsel for Dr. Martin Luther King Jr.

Constance Baker Motley is sworn in as the first African American woman in the New York State Senate.

Motley's career is marked by firsts. In 1964, she became the first African American woman in the U.S. Senate. The next year, she completed her term in the New York Senate and was elected the first female president of the New York borough of Manhattan. She used her position to confront segregation in the public school system. President Lyndon B. Johnson recognized Motley's accomplishments, and in 1966, amid staunch opposition, he nominated her as a federal judge. Motley became a U.S. District Court Judge for the Southern District of New York—and the highest-paid African American woman in government.

Motley's positive outlook and dedication sealed her success. "As she grew," her fellow judge Kimba Wood once said, "she was unfailingly optimistic and positive. She never let herself be diverted from her goal of achieving civil rights, even though, as she developed as a lawyer, she faced almost constant condescension from our profession due to her being an African American woman."

Motley's autobiography, *Equal Justice under Law: The Life of a Pioneer for Black Civil Rights and Women's Rights,* was published in 1988. It chronicles her life and many of the most significant moments in civil rights history.

AVON NYANZA WILLIAMS JR.

ATTORNEY

(1921–1994)

You can't keep on smiling at a person and not evoke a smile. You can't keep on loving a person and not evoke love. But hate doesn't have to evoke hate. . . . If you love you never accept hate.

Avon Nyanza Williams Jr. was born in Knoxville, Tennessee, on December 22, 1921. The famous civil rights attorney Thurgood Marshall was his cousin and a major inspiration. Williams determined that he too would use the legal system to make America a better place for African Americans.

Williams received his law degree from Boston University in 1947. Hungry for more education, he earned his master of law degree in 1948. He went to work as an intern for the great civil rights lawyer Zephaniah Alexander Looby in Nashville, Tennessee. This experience inspired

Williams to dedicate his career to civil rights. It also helped him decide to work for his local community rather than on the national level, as his cousin Marshall was doing.

In 1948, Williams set up his own law practice in his hometown of Knoxville, Tennessee. That same year, he filed his first civil rights lawsuit. Four students had been denied admission to the University of Tennessee graduate school because they were black. Williams took the lawsuit of *Gray v. The University of Tennessee* to the U.S. Supreme Court. The Court's decision forced the school to change its policy and admit the students.

This first case was early evidence of Williams's brilliance. In less than a year of practice, he had single-handedly won a desegregation case before the U.S. Supreme Court. A year later, in 1950, he joined Looby, attorney Carl Cowan, and his cousin Thurgood Marshall in Tennessee's first public school desegregation case. Although the men won the case, the school board delayed the admission of students so that it could, it claimed, develop a plan for integration. Many public and private institutions made this claim to keep from obeying the law indefinitely.

In 1954, the U.S. Supreme Court decision in *Brown v. Board of Education* set an important precedent. Lawyers across the nation could now challenge school systems that kept black children in separate, ill-equipped schools. Looby and Williams filed many such lawsuits and often worked for free to improve the quality of education for black children.

One such case, *Kelly v. The Nashville Board of Education,* became the longest-running lawsuit in American history. The Nashville school system continued to delay integration, and Looby and Williams continued to demand that they comply with the Court's decision. The case, which began in 1957, continued for thirty years. During this time, white parents sent their children to private schools rather than allow them to attend a school that would admit black children.

Students at Howard University during a protest in 1968

In 1953, Looby convinced Williams to join his law firm in Nashville. Together, the two men were a powerful team. Throughout the 1950s and 1960s, they took on many civil rights cases across the state of Tennessee. These cases involved school segregation, unequal pay for black employees, housing discrimination, and police brutality against African Americans.

In the 1960s, college students across the country became active in the civil rights movement. They staged sit-ins, boycotts, and protest marches. The students of the three black colleges in Nashville were especially effective because they had the full support of the black community—from the wealthy to the working class. Businessmen raised money to bail the students out of jail when they were arrested for refusing to leave a "whites only" restaurant. Lawyers represented them without charging their usual fees, and others supported the students in any way they could.

Williams advised the student leaders and worked tirelessly in court on their behalf. As a result, seven restaurants in downtown Nashville allowed blacks and whites to sit and eat together—a tremendous accomplishment in a major Southern city at that time.

Williams served in the state senate from 1968 until 1990 and had a great impact on the laws and government of Tennessee. He wrote bills that required schools to include classes on Afro-American studies, put guidance counselors in all elementary schools, and forced utility companies to provide adequate water supplies to black neighborhoods.

In 1968, in one of Williams's greatest legal victories, he persuaded the court to combine the downtown campus of the University of Tennessee in Nashville with the historically black Tennessee State University. For the first time in U.S. history, a major white university was brought under the leadership and control of a black university. In 1970, the campus of the University of Tennessee in Nashville was renamed the Avon Williams campus of Tennessee State University.

During his career, Williams received many threats and endured the anger and insults of racists. Throughout 1961, he was harassed because of his work in civil rights. His phone would often ring in the middle of the night, and the caller would shout racial slurs and threaten to kill him. Despite the danger, Williams refused to give in to hatred. He knew what he was doing was right.

After Williams's death in 1994, Tennessee governor Ned McWherter praised him as "a man of courage, conviction and conscience. He used the law as a tool to open doors of opportunity for those whose opportunities were limited."

FRED LEE SHUTTLESWORTH

CIVIL RIGHTS LEADER, COFOUNDER OF SCLC

(1922–)

It is my conviction that it is our duty and right to move courageously against Segregation: to attack it rather than waiting to defend ourselves; it is the problem of others to defend it if they can.

Fred Lee Shuttlesworth was born on March 18, 1922, in the rural town of Muglar, Alabama. He began to preach shortly after he graduated from high school and was appointed pastor of the Birmingham Bethel Baptist Church the next year.

In 1956, the year that Alabama made it illegal to be a member of the National Association for the Advancement of Colored People (NAACP), Shuttlesworth started the Alabama Christian Movement for Human Rights. He was also one of the founders of the Southern Christian Leadership Conference (SCLC) and served as the organization's first secretary. Dr. Martin Luther King Jr. once described him as "the most courageous civil rights fighter in the South."

For years, Shuttlesworth was the lone voice for civil rights in Birmingham. His home was bombed twice. A mob whipped him with chains after he tried to enroll his children in an all-white school. He was also arrested several times. He would confront anyone for the cause of civil rights, even the SCLC and its leader, Dr. King. Shuttlesworth criticized the SCLC for not being active enough in Alabama.

Amid constant personal threats, Shuttlesworth attacked segregation everywhere—in the police force, on buses, in bus terminals, schools, and public places. He was the only one bold enough to stand up to Theophilus Eugene "Bull" Connor, Alabama's commissioner of public safety and an outspoken segregationist. Shuttlesworth sued Bull Connor and the police chief, representing himself so he could cross-examine his opponents.

In 1961, Shuttlesworth moved to Cincinnati, Ohio, to become pastor of Revelation Baptist Church, but when the SCLC decided to become more active in his home state of Alabama, King and the SCLC leaders asked him to help construct a plan. Their plan was called Project C, and the C stood for confrontation. In 1963, Shuttlesworth, Ralph Abernathy, and Dr. King led a series of sit-ins and made a list of demands called the Birmingham Manifesto. The group's goal was to overcrowd the jails and create a crisis situation that the city would have to address.

After the controversial decision to include children in the protests, the jails overflowed. "I knew we were winning," he said, "when I went to court and the judge couldn't sentence me. He said, 'Mr. Shuttlesworth, I regret that because of the overcrowded condition at jail, we have no place to put you.' I said, 'Your honor, we're making progress.'"

Shuttlesworth, King, and Abernathy were listed on a court order initiated by Bull Connor. The order banned 133 civil rights leaders from participation in any demonstrations, sit-ins, or pickets. The next day, Shuttlesworth defied the order, participated in a march, and was hospitalized with a cracked rib. Despite urging from President John F. Kennedy, Shuttlesworth and the other leaders repeated the process the next day. This time, they had more than one thousand volunteers.

Connor arrived with police dogs and instructed the fire department to open their high-pressure fire hoses on the crowd. The televised images of children being knocked down, pushed into curbs, blown over cars, and attacked by Connor's dogs shocked America and outraged Birmingham's African American community. Shuttlesworth and the SCLC saw that the demonstrations would only lead to more violence, so they discontinued them. However, Project C began a conversation in Congress that ultimately led to increased civil rights legislation.

Back in Cincinnati, Shuttlesworth organized the Greater Light Baptist Church. He joined other African American ministers to help the city elect its first black mayor. He also worked to increase minority representation on the city council. In 1998, with one hundred thousand dollars of his own money, he started the Shuttlesworth Housing Foundation, which provides grants to low-income families that would otherwise be unable to purchase a home. Shuttlesworth retired from the pulpit in 2006, on his eighty-fourth birthday.

ERNEST C. WITHERS

PHOTOGRAPHER

(1922–)

My basic theory in photography is, "Is it true?"
"Does it hurt?" "What good does it do?"

The photography of Ernest Withers opened the minds and hearts of many Americans. Through his images, they witnessed the horror of the murder of young Emmett Till in Money, Mississippi. The historic photographs of the battered child, who was kidnapped and tortured by white segregationists, propelled the civil rights movement. Withers was among four photographers allowed to record the weeklong trial. He published a pamphlet said to be "the first and only complete, factual story of the Till case," which he sold for one dollar to thousands of people.

Even as a child, Withers always had a knack for being in the right place with his camera. When he was a teenager, he borrowed his sister's camera to photograph the wife of famed boxer Joe Louis, who was visiting his high school. The photo was published in the local African American newspaper, the *Tri-State Defender*. After that, he took every opportunity to fine-tune his craft.

In 1942, Withers married, and the next year, he enlisted in the U.S. Army. As a military photographer, he learned how to shoot with a large-format camera, process film in a darkroom, and make prints. While he was stationed in the South Pacific, he started a commercial photography business.

When Withers returned to Memphis, Tennessee, he continued to document his surroundings. He captured moments in the rich African American culture in Memphis—school pictures, family portraits, debutant balls, and funerals. He also photographed the Negro Leagues' Memphis Red Sox and sold prints to the fans.

In 1948, Withers became one of the first African American members of the Memphis city police force. There was a great deal of racial tension around the hiring of African American officers, who were only allowed to arrest black suspects. In 1951, Withers was falsely accused of taking money from bootleggers and was fired. The other African American officers were forced to resign. Fortunately, Withers still had his photography business, and he began to document one of the most significant periods in American history.

It was dangerous for an African American photographer to travel through the Deep South. Withers was beaten by a police officer in Jackson, Mississippi, and arrested while photographing the funeral of a civil rights activist. He worked with journalist Dorothy Gilliam to cover James Meredith's first day as a student at the University of Mississippi, which sparked riots that caused two deaths. Withers did not work with a telephoto lens, so he was often only a few feet away from the action.

After the successful Montgomery Bus Boycott, Withers recorded Dr. Martin Luther King Jr.'s first ride at the front of the newly integrated bus.

He developed close relationships with civil rights leaders and often traveled with them to record some of their most private moments. Withers also photographed King reading a news story about James Meredith's March Against Fear while King lay in bed at the Lorraine Motel in Memphis, the motel where he was later assassinated.

One of Withers's most famous photographs is of several hundred Memphis sanitation workers on strike. They are wearing hand-painted boards that read "I Am a Man," which Withers himself helped to make. This photo is one of the most widely reproduced images of the civil rights era.

White photographers did not have the same access to the inner workings of the movement as black photographers did. Withers would sell rolls of his film to white photographers for large sums of money. As a result, he did not receive credit for all of the amazing images he captured.

"Pictures tell the story" was the motto printed on Withers's business cards. With his images, he captured the struggles and triumphs of the civil rights movement. He also recorded the musical culture of historic Beale Street, where he opened his studio in the 1940s. Legendary performers B. B. King, Al Green, Isaac Hayes, and Elvis Presley are among the many celebrated figures Withers has photographed. His work has appeared in top publications, such as *Time, Newsweek, Ebony, Jet,* the *New York Times,* the *Washington Post,* and the *Chicago Defender.* It was also featured in the PBS television documentary *Eyes on the Prize* about the civil war movement and in touring exhibitions throughout the country.

Withers was inducted into the Black Press Hall of Fame and awarded an honorary doctoral degree from the Massachusetts College of Art. His body of work includes more than five million photographs. The memorable images he captured changed the heart of America.

AARON HENRY

CIVIL RIGHTS LEADER, MISSISSIPPI

(1922–1997)

Although we don't get all we pay for in this life, we certainly are not going to get anything if we don't pay.

Aaron Henry was born in Coahoma County, Mississippi, on July 2, 1922. His parents were sharecroppers who made certain that their son received a high school education. While in high school, Henry joined the National Association for the Advancement of Colored People (NAACP) as a junior member. After graduation, he enlisted in the army, and wherever he was stationed, he always made contact with a local NAACP chapter. With the help of the government's G.I. Bill of Rights, which gave money to soldiers returning from service, Henry attended the historically black Xavier University in New Orleans, Louisiana. He graduated with a degree in pharmacy.

When Henry returned home in 1950, Coahoma County was plagued with racist violence—police brutality, rapes, and countless murders of African Americans. In 1952, with R. L. Drew, H. Y. Hackett, Leola Guest, and other civil rights activists, Henry helped to establish the Clarksdale, Mississippi, chapter of the NAACP and became its first president. By 1959, he was president of the state chapter.

In 1961, several stores in Clarksdale refused to hire black workers and discriminated against black customers. Henry organized a boycott of the stores, for which he and six others were arrested. He appealed the case, and the charges were later dropped. Shortly afterward, Henry was sued for eighty thousand dollars on a sexual harassment charge. He ultimately won the case, but his pharmacy and home were firebombed, and his wife was fired from her job as a public school teacher.

In 1962, local civil rights groups in Mississippi formed the Council of Federated Organizations (COFO), and Henry was named chairman. COFO's first project was the Freedom Vote, which was designed to give African Americans practice casting ballots. In a mock election, Henry and his running mate, Ed King, generated more than ninety thousand votes throughout the state.

As state president of the NAACP, Henry worked closely with civil rights leader Medgar Evers, who was an NAACP field director for the state of Mississippi. In 1963, the two men had prepared testimony in support of the Civil Rights Act, which they planned to present to the House Judiciary Committee. Before they headed to Washington, D.C., however, Henry was flying to Houston, Texas, to address the National Pharmaceutical Association, of which he was president. The men were going to meet immediately afterward in Washington to offer their testimony. Evers drove Henry to the airport, but when he returned home, he was shot and killed in his driveway.

Henry did not learn that Evers was dead until the following morning, when he turned on his television to watch Lena Horne's appearance on the

Today Show. Horne had just performed at an event organized by Evers and was scheduled to discuss the movement in Mississippi. When Henry saw Roy Wilkins, national secretary of the NAACP, with Horne on the set—and a picture of Evers displayed at the bottom of the screen—he realized his friend was dead. Henry went on to Washington to deliver Evers's written speech and his own testimony. The Civil Rights Act was passed in 1964.

During the famous Freedom Summer of 1964, nearly one thousand white college students arrived in Mississippi to help African Americans register to vote and to assist with health care and legal aid. Henry believed that summer helped shape the attitudes of many African Americans in Mississippi. "And many a black took heart from this movement and just learned for themselves by living with whites that there are some dumb white folks and some smart white folks, just like there are some dumb black folks and some smart black folks, but that the color of the man's skin didn't make the difference," he explained.

Henry was one of the founders of the Mississippi Freedom Democratic Party (MFDP) in 1964. He was among the delegation of sixty-eight people who challenged the legality of the all-white Mississippi delegation at the Democratic National Convention. At the convention, President Lyndon B. Johnson was to be chosen to run for reelection, and hoping to avoid controversy, he proposed a way to include members of the MFDP in the convention. Under Johnson's proposal, Henry and Ed King, a white chaplain from the historically black Tougaloo College, were the only two delegates offered seats on the convention floor. "You say, Ed and Aaron can get in," said Henry, referring to himself, "but the other sixty-two can't. This is typical white man picking black folks' leaders, and that day is just gone."

The MFDP rejected the two-seat compromise and continued their fight in private hearings at a nearby hotel. The convention members put the compromise to a vote. Johnson sent his allies to threaten delegates at the

Aaron Henry holds a microphone as the father of slain civil rights worker Michael Schwerner speaks outside the Democratic National Convention in 1964.

convention into supporting the two-seat offer, so the compromise passed—but the MFDP could still claim success. That was the last year that an all-white delegation ever represented the citizens of Mississippi.

As the mood of the civil rights movement began to shift in the mid-1960s, Henry believed the MFDP had become too radical, so he created the Loyalist Democrats. He chaired their delegations to the 1968 and 1972 Democratic National Conventions. He later merged the Loyalist Democrats with the national Democratic Party.

The state of Mississippi declared April 12, 1970, Aaron Henry Day. Henry was presented with the NAACP state award for twenty years of dedicated service. On July 2, 1970, he received the Abraham Lincoln Award from the National Education Association Center for Human Relations. In 1982, he was elected to the Mississippi House of Representatives, and he remained in office until 1996, the year before he died.

CHARLES EVERS

CIVIL RIGHTS ACTIVIST, MISSISSIPPI

(1922–)

Charles Evers was the older brother of civil rights martyr Medgar Evers. He was born on September 11, 1922, in Decatur, Mississippi. Evers described his mother as a strong Christian woman. He remembers his father as a fearless man, who urged his sons to be courageous. He told them if they looked a white man in the eye, "he won't do nothing." During the 1930s, African Americans in the South were constant targets for harassment and violence. When Charles and Medgar walked to school, the school bus drivers would purposely try to splash them with muddy water as they drove past.

Although the two brothers were very different from each other, they grew up to share a deep commitment to the civil rights movement. Charles worked alongside his younger brother to establish a local

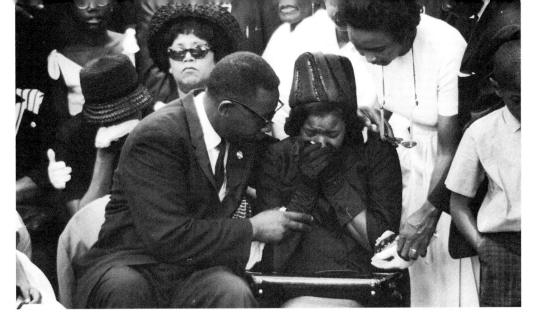

Charles Evers comforts his brother's wife at Medgar Evers's funeral.

chapter of the National Association for the Advancement of Colored People (NAACP) and became the group's voter registration chairman in 1954. After graduating from Alcorn Agricultural and Mechanical College (now Alcorn State University), he worked a number of jobs—dishwasher, cotton picker, short-order cook, and bootlegger.

Charles's political activities and business endeavors eventually got him in trouble, and he was forced to move to Chicago, Illinois, in 1956. There he continued his illegal business. "That was one way to survive," he said. "I did what I could to stay off welfare." He visited his younger brother regularly and often sent money to support the movement in Mississippi.

After Medgar was assassinated in 1963, Charles picked up where his brother left off. "I left him when I should have stayed there with him," he said. "If I had been there, he wouldn't have gotten shot because I always carry protection. I regret that. That's why I've done all I can to ensure that he didn't die in vain."

Evers assumed the position of field director for the Mississippi chapter of the NAACP. "No blacks were registered to vote when Medgar was killed, and after he was killed I went back to Mississippi to kill someone. But instead,

I decided to get into voter registration and economic power." Evers also led campaigns to support friends John F. Kennedy and Robert F. Kennedy. Throughout his career, Evers served as an unofficial adviser to politicians, including presidents Lyndon B. Johnson and Ronald Reagan, Senator Robert F. Kennedy, and Governor George Wallace.

Evers wrote his autobiography in 1970. Later, he wrote a second book, *Have No Fear,* which chronicled his and his brother's lives. The *Oakland Post* described the book as "one of the most honest, open and gripping books yet written about race in America." Evers said, "I wanted people to read what it was like for black folks in particular during the years that we came up. Many obstacles and hardships, the cruelty of racism and bigotry that many people suffered from because of the ignorant leaders."

Charles Evers was the first African American to be elected to the office of mayor in Mississippi since the period following the Civil War. As mayor of Fayette, Mississippi, he brought dignity to the small town. He paved the sidewalks in African Americans' neighborhoods. He urged General Motors to open a plant in Mississippi, which created hundreds of jobs. He ran Fayette's only doctor, who was a racist, out of town and brought in twelve doctors from the University of Michigan to train more health care professionals. He also ran an unsuccessful race for Congress and for governor of Mississippi. He eventually left the Democratic Party and joined the Republican Party to keep a watchful eye on those in power.

Because of his fearlessness and willingness to carry on the work of his brother, Mississippi is a better place for African Americans. He once said, "Any time you can put a white man in jail for life for the killing of a black man in Mississippi, it's a big change, especially when the judge is white, and also the D. A. [district attorney]. It shows that time has brought about change, as well as changing attitudes of whites, some of whom had been with us all of the time."

MAE BERTHA CARTER

Civil Rights Activist, Mississippi
(1923–1999)

I always would say to myself, 'Well, bein' black, that's a disadvantage—just bein' black—but, being uneducated, that's another disadvantage.' So, I couldn't change the black, but we certainly could change and get a good education for our kids. I was willing to die for this.

Mae Bertha Carter believed that the only way out of poverty was through education. She and her husband were sharecroppers in Sunflower County, Mississippi, in the small, rural community of Drew. They earned thirty cents an hour picking cotton.

Drew was infamous for its racial violence. It was home of the notoriously racist Senator James Eastland and the birthplace of the oppressive White Citizens' Council. African Americans feared losing their jobs, their homes, or even their lives if they integrated.

At that time, it was difficult for an African American child to get an education. The schools set aside for African Americans had poor conditions, old books, and unqualified teachers. The schools were closed during the fall and spring months so the children could work in the cotton fields.

After the Civil Rights Act of 1964, the state of Mississippi had to design a plan to integrate the schools. They created the Freedom of Choice plan, which allowed African American parents to enroll their children in schools that had historically been all white. No one in Sunflower County signed up for the plan—except the Carters. They had thirteen children, and seven of them were old enough to attend elementary through high school. The Carter children were willing to endure racism and harassment for a chance at a life that did not include picking cotton.

In August 1965, as the seven children arrived by bus for their first day of school, hecklers shouted from the streets, "Go back to your own schools, niggers." The Federal Bureau of Investigation sent agents to monitor the tense situation. For one week, the agents accompanied the local police who escorted the bus that carried the Carter children to Drew High School and A. W. James Elementary School.

African Americans in the community thought the Carters were crazy. White segregationists believed their threats and violence would convince the family to back down and remove their children from the school. The Carters never considered quitting. All seven children returned to school day after day.

White segregationists took action. That fall, they plowed up the Carters' cotton crop before the harvest and fired gunshots at their house. They called the children names and spat on them. One of the children's history teachers repeatedly referred to African Americans as "niggers" during her lessons. Gloria Carter later said, "It was shocking to go to a classroom and to sit down and then everybody pushes their desks aside and says, 'I don't want to sit by you.'"

The Carters were eventually evicted from the plantation and had trouble getting work in Drew. When other African American families began to integrate the Sunflower County schools, white families put their children in private schools, reducing the public schools' resources and funds. These events only made Mae Bertha more determined. She sued the state of Mississippi for their failed Freedom of Choice plan and worked tirelessly as a civil rights activist.

Eight of the Carter children graduated from Drew High School. Seven of them earned business degrees at the University of Mississippi in Oxford. Mae Bertha, who had been a member of the National Association for the Advancement of Colored People (NAACP) since 1955, remained very active. She also became a leader in Sunflower County's Head Start program, a government program started in 1965 to help low-income families that had preschool children.

A teacher reads to children in a Head Start classroom.

Over the years, Constance Curry, with the American Friends Service Committee, had offered encouragement and support for the Carters' efforts to integrate the schools. In 1995, she published a biography of Mae Bertha Carter called *Silver Rights*. Curry said the title represented the way that illiterate African Americans pronounced the words "civil rights." The book also contains correspondence between Curry and Carter, which chronicles the family's experience with the Mississippi public schools. The two women traveled across the country sharing the little-known story of the Carter family's heroism.

Carter's dreams were not just for her own children. In the 1990s, students in the Drew schools still suffered. Teachers were underpaid, and the schools claimed to have no funds. Carter persisted in her efforts to make Mississippi live up to its responsibility to educate its youth and prepare them to succeed in the world. She wrote letters and exposed fraud in the system. She also worked hard to find teachers and librarians, despite a shortage of qualified professionals.

In 1999, when Mae Bertha Carter died of cancer, her funeral service was held at a school that had been previously open to whites only. "I know I won't be here a thousand years," she once said. "I may not be here one year. But ain't nobody going back to slavery. And if that be what they think, they can forget it. They crazy. All the slave people who say yessir and yessir and yessir are dead. Ain't gon be no more slaves."

CORDY TINDELL VIVIAN

CIVIL RIGHTS ACTIVIST, TENNESSEE

(1924–)

I think it has to be seen, that every black person, with rare exception, has one agenda, and that's how to get rid of racism, because that's the central problem of our lives. . . . How is it possible? Will it be effective? . . . Those are the kinds of questions that we all wanted to answer.

Cordy Tindell Vivian was born in Howard, Missouri, on July 28, 1924. He and his mother moved to Macomb, Illinois, where he attended elementary school and high school. Skilled with words, Vivian became the editor of the sports section of the Western Illinois University student newspaper in Macomb. In nearby Peoria in 1947, Vivian took part in sit-in demonstrations that helped to desegregate Barton's Cafeteria, which launched his fight for civil rights.

In February 1957, Vivian worked with local leaders to form the Nashville Christian

Leadership Conference (NCLC). The NCLC was a local affiliate of the Southern Christian Leadership Conference (SCLC), which was headquartered in Atlanta, Georgia, and led by Dr. Martin Luther King Jr. and Ella Baker. The SCLC believed that, in a democratic society, all citizens had to have civil rights. The organization's members also believed the best chance for gaining those rights was through direct action and nonviolent protest for change.

In 1959, while studying for the ministry at American Baptist College in Nashville, Tennessee, Vivian met Rev. James Lawson, who was teaching the strategies of nonviolent change to students there. Vivian spoke with NCLC leaders and arranged for Lawson and Glen Smiley to teach workshops to church members and students from the many black colleges and universities of Nashville. The workshop leaders would share the successful strategies of Indian leader Mohandas Gandhi and organize a nonviolent campaign against segregation.

In February 1960, the first goal was to desegregate downtown Nashville. After three months of sit-ins, beatings, arrests, and a four-thousand-strong march to the mayor's office, the protesters succeeded. "Nonviolence made the difference," Vivian said. The students had learned at the workshops how to "begin to take the blow—cigarettes put out on you, the fact that you were being spit on—and still, still respond with some sense of dignity and with a loving concept of what you were about."

Vivian and other leaders of the student sit-in movement in Nashville continued their efforts. In 1961, when the Freedom Riders were savagely beaten and hospitalized, Vivian and others raced to Montgomery, Alabama, to take their places and continue the protest against segregated travel. The Nashville riders continued on to Jackson, Mississippi, but there they were arrested and jailed for violating local laws.

Vivian later rose in the ranks of the SCLC and worked closely with Dr. King. In 1963, King appointed him the national director of affiliates.

Vivian traveled throughout the South as an adviser on issues of nonviolence, organizing local protests, marches, and voter registration drives.

In 1965, during one such campaign in Selma, Alabama, Vivian confronted Sheriff Jim Clark on the steps of the Selma courthouse. Clark was known for forcefully keeping African Americans from voting in Selma elections. Vivian told him, "This is not a local problem. This is a national problem. You cannot keep anyone in the United States from voting without hurting the rights of all other citizens. Democracy is built on this." A news camera was filming when Clark punched Vivian in the face and knocked him down. The scene aired on television stations across the nation, shocking many Americans, who were unaware of the racism that was commonplace in the South.

In 1965, Vivian, who believed that higher education was a necessary step for empowerment, started a program called Vision, which provided college scholarships for more than seven hundred students in Alabama. Today, the program is called Upward Bound.

Although the civil rights movement changed its methods after 1969, Vivian and others continued to gather together, organize protests, and work through local and national government institutions. In 1969, he wrote *Black Power and the American Myth.* It was the first book of the modern-day civil rights movement.

MEDGAR EVERS

CIVIL RIGHTS LEADER

(1925–1963)

You can kill a man but you can't kill an idea.

Medgar Evers was born on July 2, 1925, in Decatur, Mississippi. He grew up witnessing unspeakable acts of suffering and brutality. "I used to watch the Saturday night sport of white men trying to run down a Negro with their car, or white gangs coming through town to beat up a Negro," he said. Evers was inspired by his father, James, who was proud and unafraid. "He wouldn't step off the sidewalk for anyone."

Determined to earn his high school diploma, Evers walked 12 miles (19.3 km) each way to attend school. After graduation in 1943, he joined the U.S. Army and served in Normandy, France, during World War II. He had never before been outside of Mississippi or the confines of the racist Jim Crow laws of the South.

With an honorable discharge, Evers returned to Mississippi only to discover that he was still considered a boy, not a man, and was treated disrespectfully. His brother, Charlie, talked him into registering to vote in an upcoming election. The Evers brothers and four other black men registered at the courthouse, but when they returned on the day of the election, a gang of segregationists threatened them with guns and knives. They left without casting their ballots.

Evers attended the historically black Alcorn State University (which was then called Alcorn Agricultural and Mechanical College), where he majored in business administration. He played football, ran track, sang in the college choir, and argued for the debate team. Evers was a natural leader. He held several student offices and worked as editor of the campus newspaper. He also became active with the National Association for the Advancement of Colored People (NAACP).

In 1950, Evers met Myrlie Beasely, who also attended Alcorn. They married the next year, and after Evers graduated, they moved to Mound Bayou, Mississippi. There Evers worked as an insurance salesman. When he made sales calls to the poor, rural homes in the Mississippi Delta, he saw the changes that needed to take place in order for African American families to succeed in Mississippi. He soon became politically active. He organized boycotts of gas stations that refused to allow African Americans to use the restrooms. He also recruited members and set up new chapters of the NAACP.

Evers eventually quit his insurance job to dedicate himself full-time to the civil rights movement. Organizing Mississippi's black citizens to take action was a tough job. The NAACP local membership had dropped greatly because so many blacks were leaving the state, and because those who remained feared the white segregationists. Despite the difficulties, Evers continued to travel door to door to discuss the need for action with state residents.

In 1954, Evers, who had long dreamed of becoming a lawyer, decided to conduct his own experiment. He applied to the all-white University of Mississippi law school in Oxford. Soon after, the U.S. Supreme Court handed down its ruling in *Brown v. Board of Education,* which made racially segregated schools unconstitutional. Evers's application was denied, and he believed he was rejected because of his race.

NAACP leaders admired Evers's dedication and courage and made him the organization's first field director in Mississippi. He moved to Jackson and opened an NAACP office. Myrlie worked by his side as secretary, and together they organized voter registration drives and boycotts. As part of his job, Evers had to investigate racial violence and the murders of African Americans. These reports would help the NAACP to document in court the many incidents in which the civil rights of African Americans were being violated. When Emmett Till was murdered in 1955, Evers traveled to the town of Money to search for evidence and witnesses.

Because of his work, Evers and his family were always in danger. They received threatening phone calls daily. Evers taught his children to drop to the floor at the sound of gunshots and crawl to the bathtub for safety. He had several guns in the house and in the car. In 1962, when Evers boycotted the segregated white merchants in downtown Jackson, his family's home was firebombed.

The boycott received national attention, as did Evers's involvement with James Meredith, who was admitted to the University of Mississippi, which had rejected Evers's application years before. In a televised speech on May 20, 1962, Evers spoke about the racial injustices and discriminatory practices that African Americans faced. The speech was so powerful it touched the hearts of some of Jackson's white citizens. The following day, white citizens called

Medgar Evers (right) and James Meredith at a press conference

the NAACP office in support of Evers's speech and segregationist signs were removed from bus depots and train stations.

Evers believed that the time was right for a major civil rights movement in Mississippi. In 1963, he wrote letters to the governor of Mississippi, the mayor of Jackson, and to the city's chamber of commerce. He promised to use all legal means to end racism and segregation in Jackson. In response, Mayor Allen Thompson urged African Americans not to support Evers or listen to any member of the NAACP or the Congress of Racial Equality (CORE), which had worked with Evers on voter registration drives.

Because of the constant danger, the Evers family had a rule to never exit the car on the driver's side. The vacant lot on that side of the house was an ideal spot for a sniper to hide. On the night of June 12, 1963, Evers pulled up to his house and, without thinking, exited from the door on the driver's side. He was shot in the back by a hidden sniper. He was rushed to University

Hospital, where the staff broke the segregation policy to admit him for emergency care, but it was too late. Evers died less than an hour later.

The death of Medgar Evers marked an emotional turning point in the civil rights movement. During the funeral procession in Jackson, four thousand mourners marched in the streets shouting, "After Medgar, No More Fear." Myrlie Evers said, "It was like a dam had burst, and people were no longer afraid." After the services in Jackson, Evers's body was taken to Arlington Cemetery in Washington, D.C., where he was buried with honors for his military service.

Moved by Evers's assassination, President John F. Kennedy asked Congress to draw up a comprehensive civil rights bill. The president never lived to sign the bill, however. In November of that same year, Kennedy was assassinated. In 1964, President Lyndon B. Johnson signed the Civil Rights Act, which finally outlawed discrimination and segregation.

Evers's assassin, Byron De La Beckwith, a member of the Ku Klux Klan, was arrested and tried twice. On both occasions, an all-white jury could not reach a unanimous decision, and De La Beckwith remained a free man. He returned home to a hero's welcome from white segregationists who lined the highway with signs celebrating their so-called victory. More than thirty years later, due to the constant efforts of Myrlie Evers, the case was reopened. In 1994, De La Beckwith was found guilty of the murder of Medgar Evers and sentenced to life in prison. He died in prison in 2001.

MALCOLM LITTLE, A.K.A. MALCOLM X, EL HAJJ MALIK EL SHABAZZ

CIVIL RIGHTS LEADER

(1925–1965)

We don't intend to break the law because when you're trying to register to vote, you're upholding the law. It's the one who tries to prevent you from registering to vote who's breaking the law. And you've got a right, you've got a right to protect yourself by any means necessary.

Malcolm Little was born on May 19, 1925, in Omaha, Nebraska. His father was a Baptist minister who supported the ideas of Marcus Garvey. Garvey's Black Nationalism promoted the unity of peoples of African descent around the globe. The Littles were forced to move several times because of death threats from a white supremacist group. Their home in Lansing, Michigan, was burned to the ground.

The course of Malcolm's life changed when his father was killed in a streetcar accident. Malcolm's mother was so overwhelmed with sadness she had an emotional breakdown and was hospitalized. The children were separated and placed in foster homes and orphanages.

In 1941, Malcolm moved to Boston to live with his half-sister. He was an excellent student, but lost interest in school when his favorite teacher dismissed his dream to become a lawyer, calling it "no realistic goal for a nigger." Little dropped out of high school and moved to Harlem, New York. Unable to find steady work and classified as unfit to serve in the army, he became a drug dealer, pimp, and leader of a gambling ring. In 1946, he was arrested in Boston and sentenced to eight to ten years in prison for his role in a burglary ring.

While he was in prison, Little read books to educate himself. His brother Reginald would visit often and talk about the Nation of Islam (NOI), which he had joined. The NOI, founded in Detroit, Michigan, is a religious group that is related to Islam, the faith of Muslims throughout the world. Members of the NOI also call themselves Black Muslims. Malcolm wanted to learn more and studied the writings of NOI leader Elijah Poole, known as the Honorable Elijah Muhammad.

Muhammad's beliefs were similar to the Black Nationalist views Malcolm's father had risked his life to support. Members of the NOI believed that African men should join together to achieve their goals. They followed strict rules regarding behavior, cleanliness, dress, and the treatment of women. The group supported the racial and economic separation of African Americans and whites, who were believed to be demons. In the NOI tradition, Malcolm dropped his "slave name," the family name Little, which belonged to his ancestors' slave masters. Malcolm Little became Malcolm X.

A crowd listens to Malcolm X speak.

In 1952, when he was released from prison, Malcolm X went to live with his brother in Detroit. The next year, he moved to Chicago to live with Elijah Muhammad. Muhammad appointed Malcolm as a minister of Islam and, in 1953, asked him to lead a temple in Boston. The next year, Malcolm moved to another temple in New York, and in 1955, to another in Philadelphia.

Malcolm X spread the message of Islam through radio broadcasts, newspaper columns, and television. His speeches stirred his audiences. He told them, "Stop sweet-talking [the white man]—tell him how you feel. Tell him . . . what kind of hell you been catching, and let him know that if he's not ready to clean his house up, he shouldn't have a house. It should catch on fire, and burn down."

The male members of the Nation of Islam were easy to identify. They wore close-cut hair, crisp suits, and bowties. They were peaceful, but if called to action, would not hesitate to protect their own. They marched in step with military precision and responded instantly to even a slight hand signal from Malcolm X.

In 1959, journalist Mike Wallace produced a documentary about the Nation of Islam entitled *The Hate That Produced Hate.* He interviewed Malcolm X and named him one of the most powerful leaders in the country. During the interview, Malcolm X revealed details of Elijah Muhammad's private life and angered other members of the NOI. Still, Malcolm X continued to travel throughout the world as the group's representative. He was interviewed by African American writer James Baldwin and joined debates at Harvard, Howard, and Columbia universities. The *New York Times* named him the second most sought-after speaker in America. Membership in the NOI increased dramatically—from five hundred in 1952 to thirty thousand in 1963—largely due to the influence of Malcolm X.

Some people believed that Malcolm X preached the opinions that many African Americans were to afraid to express. White Americans and civil rights leaders, such as Roy Wilkins and Dr. Martin Luther King Jr., feared that Malcolm's strong, militant messages would lead to violence. The NOI believed that the fame of Malcolm X had overshadowed the leadership of Elijah Muhammad. The federal government considered Malcolm X a threat to national security. The Federal Bureau of Investigation (FBI) planted surveillance devices in Malcolm's phone, home, and office to monitor his activities.

In 1963, when President John F. Kennedy was shot and killed, Malcolm X shocked the nation with his public statement that the assassination was a case of "the chickens coming home to roost." Elijah Muhammad officially silenced Malcolm for ninety days. Malcolm suspected, however, that the leader's harsh action toward him was caused by something else. That same year, Malcolm X had discovered that Elijah Muhammad had had several secret love affairs and fathered illegitimate children, a practice that violated the NOI's strict teachings and high moral standards.

Malcolm X felt betrayed and left the NOI in 1964 to found his own organization, the Muslim Mosque, Inc. Soon after, he left the country in a pilgrimage to the holy city of Mecca in Saudi Arabia. There he witnessed Muslims of all races united in prayer together. This experience changed his opinion about white people and the separatist views he had long embraced. Malcolm X returned to the United States, having taken the name El Hajj Malik El Shabazz. He announced, "In the past, yes, I have made sweeping indictments of all white people. I will never be guilty of that again—as I know now that some white people are truly sincere, that some truly are capable of being brotherly toward a black man. The true Islam has shown me that a blanket indictment of all white people is as wrong as when whites make blanket indictments against blacks." In 1965, he formed the Organization of Afro-American Unity to advance the civil rights movement with his new vision of humanity.

Malcolm X had heard reports that the NOI wanted him dead. On February 14, 1965, his house was firebombed. One week later, while giving a speech at the Manhattan Audubon Ballroom, he was shot and killed by three gunmen. The three, who were arrested, were members of the NOI.

Fifteen hundred mourners attended the funeral for Malcolm X in Harlem on February 27, 1965. Actor, activist, and friend Ossie Davis delivered the eulogy:

Many will ask what Harlem finds to honor in this stormy, controversial and bold young captain. . . . And we will answer and say to them: Did you ever talk to Brother Malcolm? Did you ever touch him, or have him smile at you? Did you ever really listen to him? . . . For if you did you would know him. And if you knew him you would know why we must honor him.

RALPH ABERNATHY

CIVIL RIGHTS LEADER
(1926–1990)

I tried to be that consoling force always with him and supporting the ministry and the work of Martin Luther King. He was my Paul, and I was his Timothy. And we worked hand in hand.

The Reverend Ralph Abernathy was the trusted and constant companion of Dr. Martin Luther King Jr. Abernathy was born on March 11, 1926. He was the son of a well-to-do farmer in Linden, Alabama, but he had no interest in farming. When he returned from serving in the army after World War II, he enrolled in Alabama State University, in Montgomery, where he began his work as a political activist.

The school was run-down, with little or no heat or hot water in the dormitories. Abernathy started a campaign to protest the poor living conditions on campus. He majored in mathematics but soon realized

Ralph Abernathy (left) and Martin Luther King Jr. (center) during a protest in Albany, New York

he wanted to dedicate his life to the ministry. In 1948, he became an ordained minister. In 1950, he graduated from Alabama State and then went on to earn a graduate degree in sociology from Atlanta University. Shortly after graduation, he became pastor of the First Baptist Church in Montgomery.

Abernathy met Dr. King in the early days of the Montgomery Bus Boycott. A group of local ministers and activists agreed to support the boycott protesting segregated transportation. They decided to form a new organization, which Abernathy named the Montgomery Improvement Association (MIA).

Abernathy tried to get King involved in the civil rights movement, but King was busy with his new position as minister of the Dexter Avenue Baptist Church. Rufus Lewis—who owned a private nightclub that only admitted African Americans who were registered to vote—was a member of the Dexter Avenue church. Lewis knew King was a powerful speaker, and he suggested that Abernathy and Edgar Daniel "E. D." Nixon convince King to lead the MIA.

With King as its chairman, the newly formed MIA held a meeting at the Holt Street Baptist Church and invited the community to join them. More than five thousand people gathered at the church to decide if they wanted to continue the bus boycott. Abernathy said, "The fear left. The fear that had shackled us across the years all left suddenly when we were in that church together."

From that point on, Abernathy and King were inseparable. The two men, who were the same height and weight, came to be known as the Civil Rights Twins. "Even when we were not together in prison, we were together in spirit. We thought alike," Abernathy said. On April 4, 1968, when King was shot by a sniper's bullet on the balcony of the Lorraine Motel in Memphis, Tennessee, Abernathy held his dying friend in his arms and assured him. "Martin, don't worry," he said, "it will be alright."

After King's death, Abernathy assumed leadership as president of the Southern Christian Leadership Conference (SCLC). His first order of business was to carry out King's Poor People's Campaign. The purpose of the 1968 campaign was to expose the struggles facing America's poor. An interracial community of demonstrators built and lived in huts near the Lincoln Memorial in Washington, D.C. The temporary "town" became known as Resurrection City, U.S.A. When Abernathy refused to remove the huts as instructed by police, he was arrested and jailed for three weeks.

Abernathy led the SCLC for ten years through one of its most difficult periods. With King no longer in charge, some SCLC members wanted to make changes in the organization. During the 1970s, as Stokely Carmichael's Black Power movement grew, differences arose between the more conservative and the more militant members of the SCLC.

In 1977, Abernathy left the SCLC. In 1988, he published his autobiography, *And the Walls Came Tumbling Down.* Abernathy continued to serve as pastor of the West Hunter Baptist Church in Atlanta until his death in 1990.

HOSEA WILLIAMS

CIVIL RIGHTS ACTIVIST AND ORGANIZER
(1926–2000)

Unbossed and unbought!

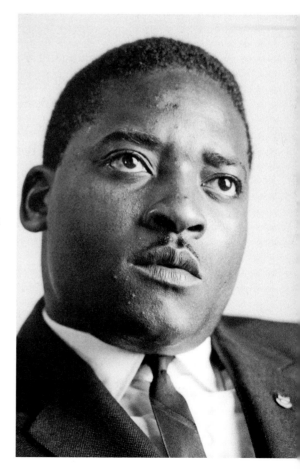

Hosea Williams lived a life of close calls and near misses. At the age of thirteen, he was attacked and almost lynched by a white mob for being too friendly with a local white girl. He described himself during his early days as a thug, a gangster, and a gambler. He quickly tired of jobs he'd held as a dishwasher, janitor, and farmworker.

In 1942, at the age of sixteen, Williams lied about his age and enlisted in the U.S. Army. For four years, he served as a weapons carrier in an all-black unit stationed in Europe. A Nazi bomb went off in his foxhole and killed everyone except him. He suffered serious leg injuries and was not rescued until the following day. The truck that transported him to the hospital was ambushed—and,

Martin Luther King Jr. (right) meets with Hosea Williams (center) and Andrew Young (left)

once again, everyone except Williams was killed. The young staff sergeant was released from duty with a Purple Heart, the government's medal of honor for heroism, and a cane for the permanent damage to his legs.

After his thirteen-month stay at a British hospital, Williams was on a Greyhound bus headed to his hometown of Attapulgus, Georgia. The bus stopped at a segregated bus station and Williams drank from a "whites only" drinking fountain. He was severely beaten and taken to the U.S. veterans hospital, where the doctors thought he would not live through the night. When Williams walked out of that hospital, he decided to join the National Association for the Advancement of Colored People (NAACP), an activist organization working for civil rights.

In 1947, Williams went back to school to get his high school degree. He then completed his undergraduate degree at Morris Brown College in Atlanta and went on to get a graduate degree in chemistry from the former Atlanta

University. He was hired as a chemist at the U.S. Department of Agriculture (USDA), where he met Juanita Terry. The couple married and moved to Savannah, Georgia, to start a family.

One afternoon, Williams took his two children to a drugstore in Savannah, and the course of his life changed. His children wanted to spin on the lunch counter stools, so he had to explain segregation to them. "I started crying because I realized I couldn't tell them the truth. The truth was, they were black, and they didn't allow black people to use those lunch counters. So I picked the two kids up and went back to the car, and I guess I made them a promise I'd bring them back someday."

To make good on that promise, Williams became active in the civil rights movement. He joined local sit-ins and marches. Once, he served thirty-five days in prison, where he received only bread and water. In his lifetime, Williams was arrested more than 135 times. His later arrests reflected a problem with alcohol abuse, for which he received rehabilitation treatment. His early arrests, however, were a badge of heroism.

In 1963, Dr. Martin Luther King Jr., the president of the Southern Christian Leadership Conference (SCLC), took note of Williams's efforts. He persuaded him to move to Atlanta to join his staff. According to SCLC member Tyrone Brooks, King knew Williams had courage, so King sent him into each new town to organize and mobilize the people. King would then pull Williams out and send in Andrew Young to negotiate.

From 1964 to 1965, Williams was at the center of the events that shaped the civil rights movement. Along with John Lewis, Williams led voter registration drives and organized the 1965 march from Selma to Montgomery, Alabama—the event that became known as Bloody Sunday. Marchers were asked to turn back as they crossed the Edmund Pettus Bridge. Williams asked if the group could kneel and pray first. In less than a minute, Alabama state troopers on horseback beat the protesters with nightsticks and sprayed them with tear gas. The shocking images of brutality were captured by television crews and aired throughout the world. The incident was one of the key events that prompted Congress to pass the Voting Rights Act of 1965.

In 1968, Williams accompanied King to support the successful, sixty-five-day Memphis sanitation workers' strike, which was followed two months later by King's assassination. Williams remained active with the SCLC under the leadership of Rev. Ralph Abernathy and Rev. Joseph Lowery. Later in 1968, he performed his usual duties as the national mobilizer for the late Dr. King's Poor People's Campaign.

Hosea Feed the Hungry and Homeless is a nonprofit organization in Atlanta, started by Williams in 1970. That year, he and his wife served Thanksgiving dinner in the Wheatley Baptist Church to two hundred homeless people. The foundation became well known for providing hot meals, supplies, haircuts, and other free services to people in need during the Thanksgiving and Christmas holidays. Today, more than three thousand volunteers serve more than thirty thousand meals every year in Turner Stadium in Atlanta.

In the 1970s, Williams decided to fight for equal rights from political office. He represented the Fifty-Fourth District of the Georgia state legislature from 1974 to 1985. He also served as a city councilman in 1986 and as DeKalb County commissioner from 1991 to 1994.

In 1987, Williams, a master mobilizer, organized the largest protest in the South since the 1960s. An estimated thirty thousand people marched with him through the streets of Forsyth County, Georgia, to protest the region's harassment of its predominantly African Americans residents.

In 2000, at Williams's funeral services, Congressman John Lewis said, "Hosea is more than one of the foot soldiers. He was brave, courageous and a daring individual, who had little or no fear. . . . He was the genius . . . steadfast and determined."

HAROLD "HARRY" GEORGE BELAFONTE JR.

SINGER, ACTOR, PRODUCER, ACTIVIST, AND HUMANITARIAN
(1927–)

My involvement just filled me up so much.
I couldn't wait to get up every day.

Harold George Belafonte Jr. was born on March 1, 1927, in Harlem, New York. His parents were Jamaican immigrants. As a child, he was dyslexic and struggled in the classroom. By the time he was seventeen years old, Belafonte had dropped out of high school and joined the U.S. Navy. During his tour of duty, he met African Americans who introduced him to the writings of black leader and writer W. E. B. Du Bois, who had a great influence on his life.

In 1948, Belafonte settled in New York City and joined the American Negro

Harry Belafonte (second from left) at a fundraising rally in Paris with (from right) Martin Luther King Jr., Yves Montand, and Simone Signoret

Theatre in Harlem. There he met his acting mentor, Paul Robeson, and fellow actor and activist Sidney Poitier, who became a lifelong friend. In 1953, Belafonte earned a Tony Award. The next year, he starred with Dorothy Dandridge in *Carmen Jones*, a role that launched his acting career.

Belafonte and his fellow African American entertainers seemed to have it all—money, respect, fame. When they traveled in the South, however, they could not dine or sleep in the hotels in which they performed. The Jim Crow laws of the region would not allow blacks and whites to occupy the same facilities. Belafonte decided to take a stand against segregation. From 1954 to 1961, he refused to perform in the South. This period turned out to be one of the most successful times in his career.

Belafonte's unique singing voice made him one of the most popular entertainers in the world. He brought the rhythms of the Caribbean to America, and his 1956 album, *Calypso,* became the first record to sell more than one million copies.

In 1959, the actor also became a producer. He started a company called HarBel Productions, dedicated to producing movies by and about African Americans. His first release, *Odds Against Tomorrow,* was a sharp portrayal of how people destroy each other with hate. By 1960, Belafonte had starred in several films, including the famed *Island in the Sun.* The television special *Tonight with Belafonte* made him the first African American television producer—and the first African American—to earn an Emmy Award.

Belafonte became a close friend and confidante of Dr. Martin Luther King Jr. In 1963, he sent money to bail King out of the Birmingham jail after King was arrested during a demonstration. Belafonte also provided thousands of dollars to release other jailed protesters. He helped to finance the Freedom Rides, supported voter registration drives, and provided seed money for the start of the Student Nonviolent Coordinating Committee (SNCC). He also met with King, Ossie Davis, and other activists to plan the 1963 March on Washington for Jobs and Freedom.

Along with entertainers Lena Horne, Paul Robeson, and many others, Belafonte was blacklisted and suddenly unable to get work in Hollywood. People shunned him because of his participation in the civil rights movement. Still, he did not regret his commitment to the movement: "The fact that I may have lost millions of dollars or some people wouldn't talk to me does not equate. My involvement just filled me up so much. I couldn't wait to get up every day. Still can't." Television host Ed Sullivan, a powerful man in Hollywood, requested that Belafonte's name finally be removed from the blacklist.

After the civil rights movement ended in 1968, Belafonte continued to fight for human rights on a global scale. In the 1980s, his idea for the song "We Are the World" helped to raise seventy million dollars for the fight against famine in Ethiopia. He was the second American to be appointed as goodwill ambassador for the United Nations Children's Fund (UNICEF). Belafonte actively participated in the struggle to end apartheid in South

Africa and chaired the committee to welcome South African civil rights leader Nelson Mandela to the United States.

Robeson once told him, "Get them to sing your songs, and they'll want to know who you are." For forty years, Belafonte worked to put together a musical collection that celebrated his love for folk music and African culture. *The Long Road to Freedom: An Anthology of Black Music,* released in 2001, consists of eighty songs and more than fifty artists on five CDs. The collection documents the journey of black people from West Africa to slavery and beyond. "It's the beautiful sound of people who refuse to submit," Belafonte said.

In 1994, he received the National Medal of the Arts and, in 2000, the Grammy Award for Lifetime Achievement. To support future generations of creative artists, Belafonte gives a percentage of his income to the Belafonte Foundation of Music and Art.

Belafonte continues to work for peace. In 2001, after racially motivated riots broke out in Cincinnati, Ohio, he organized the Urban Peace Movement. He has taken a stance against the war in Iraq and supports ways to achieve world peace through nonviolence. He continues to follow his own advice: "Leave the world a better place than it was when you came into it."

CORETTA SCOTT KING

FIRST LADY OF THE CIVIL RIGHTS MOVEMENT

(1927–2006)

Hate is too great a burden to bear. It injures the hater more than it injures the hated.

Coretta Scott King is known as the First Lady of the Civil Rights Movement. Her grace, strength, and unwavering support for her husband, Dr. Martin Luther King Jr., her children, and the civil rights movement are legendary.

King was born in Heiberger, Alabama, on April 27, 1927. She had to walk 4 miles (6.4 km) a day to a run-down school for African American children. Her parents valued education and made sure their children received the best schooling. After she completed sixth grade, the Scotts sent Coretta to join her sister at Lincoln High School, a private, all-black school in Marion, forty miles away. The girls stayed with relatives during the week and returned to Heiberger on the weekends—until their father converted a truck so their mother could drive the girls to school each day.

Coretta loved to sing. After she graduated as valedictorian of her high school class, she enrolled at Antioch College in Ohio, where she majored in music and elementary education. While she was at Antioch, she became a member of the local chapter of the National Association for the Advancement of Colored People (NAACP). She was also a member of the Young Progressives and attended the Progressive Party convention in 1948.

After graduation from college, she moved to Boston, where she enrolled at the New England Conservatory of Music to study voice and violin. She soon met a young divinity student from Georgia who was pursuing his doctorate at Boston University. His name was Martin Luther King Jr. They talked about their desire to get involved in the peace movement and to help improve conditions for African Americans. At that time, Coretta thought her contribution would be as a singer—not as the wife of the man who would become the leader of the civil rights movement.

In 1953, the two got married on the front lawn of the Scott home. The ceremony was conducted by the Reverend Martin Luther King Sr. In 1954, after Coretta completed her degree, the couple moved to Montgomery, Alabama, where her husband had accepted the position of pastor of the Dexter Street Baptist Church. Shortly after their move, the Montgomery Bus Boycott began, and so did the civil rights movement.

As the movement grew, the couple faced constant threats. In 1956, their home was bombed by segregationists. Coretta, her baby Yolanda, and a church member were in the house at the time, but no one was hurt. "I am convinced that if I had not had a wife with the fortitude, strength and calmness of Coretta," Dr. King once said, "I could not have stood up amid the ordeals and tensions surrounding the Montgomery movement. . . . In the darkest moments she always brought the light of hope."

The King family eats lunch after attending church services, 1964.

Throughout the movement, Coretta often represented her husband and helped spread his message of nonviolent social change. She gave speeches and often accompanied him during marches and rallies. An accomplished singer, she gave Freedom Concerts to raise funds for the movement. She combined prose, poetry, and narration with musical selections.

In 1957, Coretta accompanied her husband on a monthlong journey to India. In 1959, they traveled to Ghana to celebrate that country's newly won independence. In 1964, the couple traveled to Oslo, Norway, where Dr. King received the Nobel Peace Prize.

One of Mrs. King's favorite quotes was by Horace Mann, a leader in education reform: "Be ashamed to die until you have won some victory for humanity." In 1968, just a few days after Dr. King's assassination in Memphis, Tennessee, Mrs. King led a march in support of the striking sanitation workers. She gave a passionate speech in which she encouraged them to continue their fight so as not to let her husband's death be in vain.

Coretta Scott King received more than fifty awards and honorary doctorates from more than forty universities. An ambassador for world peace, she led goodwill trips to four continents. In 1986, she participated in a protest against apartheid at the South African Embassy in Washington, D.C., for which she was arrested.

In 1983, Mrs. King organized more than seven hundred human rights groups to form the New Coalition of Conscience, which sponsored the twentieth-anniversary celebration of the historic March on Washington for Jobs and Freedom. In 1986, she fought to establish a national holiday in honor of Dr. King, which is now observed every year in January.

In 1995, after serving for twenty-seven years, she retired from her position as the director of the Martin Luther King Jr. Center for Non-Violent Social Change, which she founded in Atlanta, Georgia. She passed the leadership role on to her son, Dexter King. Then she turned her focus to AIDS education and efforts to end gun violence.

When Coretta Scott King died on January 30, 2006, Republican National Committee Chairman Ken Mehlman said, "When the voice of the movement was tragically silenced, the wife of the fallen leader took up his cause and marched forward. Coretta Scott King shared her husband's dream for an America where their children 'will not be judged by the color of their skin but by the content of their character.'"

JAMES LAWSON
Civil Rights Leader
(1928–)

Through nonviolence, courage displaces fear; love transforms hate.
Acceptance dissipates prejudice; hope ends despair.

James Lawson was born in Uniontown, Pennsylvania, on September 22, 1928. When he was four years old, the family moved to Masselin, Ohio, where his father had taken a position as minister of the St. James Methodist Church.

Lawson was raised to value love and the sanctity of life. His father carried a pistol for protection, but his mother opposed any form of violence. Lawson was taught that "birth was meant to be" and that each person has a purpose. One day, he had an experience that helped him shape his own purpose in life.

As the young boy turned the corner onto Main Street, a white boy yelled

"Nigger!" from the open window of a parked car. Lawson walked over to the car, hit the child with his fist, and went on his way. When he returned home and told his mother what had happened, she asked him, "Jimmy, what good did that do? Isn't there a better way?" In that moment, he decided to never use his fists again to settle a dispute and instead to find a "better way."

In 1947, after his high school graduation, Lawson earned his license to preach. He began reading the nonviolent teachings of the Indian leader Mohandas Gandhi. He also joined Fellowship of Reconciliation (FOR), an antiwar organization founded on the belief that love in action has the power to change unjust political, social, and economic structures.

When the Korean War began in 1950, Lawson was called into military service. He sent his draft form in with a letter explaining his beliefs against violence and his refusal to fight. He was in his senior year at Baldwin Wallace College in Brea, Ohio. In 1951, just before graduation, Lawson was arrested, tried, and imprisoned for resisting the draft. He served thirteen months of his three-year sentence and refused to take a ministerial or student deferment, which would have allowed him to go free. He considered his jail sentence a form of protest and a badge of honor.

Lawson knew Bayard Rustin and others activists who had been conscientious objectors during World War II. They had also served time in jail for their beliefs and taught Lawson how to cope while he was there. On their advice, he refused to allow the jail routine to dominate his life. If the wake-up call was at 6:00 A.M., Lawson rose at 5:00 A.M. During the regularly scheduled mealtimes, he often fasted and prayed instead. The prison had an extensive library, and he read countless books on psychology and other subjects. He became the editor of the prison newspaper and a member of the library staff.

When Lawson was released, he finished his college degree. Through a FOR program, he went to India to work as a Methodist missionary and sports coach. The Board of Missions of the Methodist Church then invited Lawson to work at Hislop College in Nagpur, India. Lawson also worked with the World Student Christian Federation and organized work camps to build homes and sewers in the villages of northeastern and central India. He met Gandhi's followers, attended conferences on nonviolence, and read more of the leader's essays and speeches that had only been published in India.

Lawson returned to the United States in 1955 to attend graduate school at Oberlin College. There he heard Dr. Martin Luther King Jr. speak. At the luncheon afterward, he told King that he would like to work in the South one day to fight segregation. King urged him not to wait, explaining that the movement needed someone with Lawson's experience in nonviolent action. Lawson left graduate school and moved to Nashville, Tennessee, where he worked as secretary of the FOR office there. He also enrolled in the Divinity School of Vanderbilt University, although he was eventually expelled for his involvement with the civil rights movement.

Dr. King and other church leaders formed the Southern Christian Leadership Conference (SCLC), an organization committed to working for social justice. Lawson talked with SCLC leaders about the teachings of Gandhi and Jesus and the history of nonviolent social change. King once described Lawson as "the leading theorist and strategist of nonviolence in the world."

In 1957, Lawson helped prepare the Little Rock Nine to face their difficult first day at a newly integrated school in Little Rock, Arkansas. He also conducted nonviolence workshops for the students of Fisk University and Tennessee State. These students later staged the successful sit-ins and boycotts that desegregated restaurants in Nashville.

Role-playing was an important part of Lawson's workshops. He would ask his students to imagine they were in a threatening situation: "You are standing on the corner waiting for the light to change, and someone you don't know walks up and slaps you. You are to respond nonviolently." His students learned to respond to violence with compassion and courage. "Once they [the

James Lawson is escorted to a police wagon in 1960.

protesters] began to enter into demonstrations and discover they could do it, they became fearless," Lawson said.

Lawson coordinated the Freedom Rides of 1961, which ended the segregation of bus and train travel. In 1966, he helped organize the completion of James Meredith's March Against Fear, when the injured Meredith could not continue. He also provided guidance and support as chairman of the strike committee during the Memphis sanitation workers' strike in 1968.

Throughout the years, Lawson has continued to speak out against racism and U.S. military actions around the world, and in support of gay and lesbian rights. Today, he fights poverty as president of Clergy and Laity United for Economic Justice. Through public demonstrations, this interfaith group advocates for the "working poor" and pressures institutions and businesses to pay employees a living wage. Lawson is also board president of the Los Angeles, California, chapter of the SCLC.

DR. MARTIN LUTHER KING JR.

CIVIL RIGHTS LEADER

(1929–1968)

Now, I say to you today my friends, even though we face the difficulties of today and tomorrow, I still have a dream. It is a dream deeply rooted in the American dream. I have a dream that one day this nation will rise up and live out the true meaning of its creed: "We hold these truths to be self-evident, that all men are created equal."

Martin Luther King Jr. was born Michael King Jr. His father, who was a minister, changed his name to Martin Luther in honor of the founder of the Lutheran church. Young Michael also took the name, although he did not plan to follow in the footsteps of his father and grandfather and become a minister, too. While he was a student at Morehouse College in Atlanta, Georgia, King attended a Bible class that sparked his faith. He was ordained a Baptist minister on February 25, 1948.

Martin Luther King Jr. rides the Montgomery bus with Rev. Glenn Smiley of Texas in 1956.

King enrolled in Crozer Theological Seminary in Chester, Pennsylvania, and then earned his doctorate in systematic theology at Boston University. In 1952, he met Coretta Scott, an aspiring singer from Alabama, while both were students in Boston. They married in 1953 and eventually had four children: Yolanda Denise, Martin Luther III, Dexter Scott, and Bernice Albertine. In 1954, King became pastor of the Dexter Avenue Baptist Church in Montgomery, Alabama.

In 1955, Rosa Parks refused to give up her seat to a white man, as required by the Jim Crow laws of Montgomery. Her arrest prompted black citizens of Montgomery to form the Montgomery Improvement Association (MIA). King was elected its president. The MIA organized a boycott of the Montgomery buses, which lasted 381 days. Finally, in 1956, the city agreed to end segregated seating on buses. Nonviolent protest had achieved the first major victory of the civil rights movement.

The success in Montgomery inspired boycotts and protests in several other Southern cities. Dr. King and other religious leaders formed the Southern Christian Leadership Conference (SCLC) to coordinate their efforts throughout the South. King was elected president. Civil rights activist Ella Baker was made director, to set up the structure and oversee the day-to-day activities. James Lawson worked to teach SCLC leaders about peaceful ways to resist violence.

The Reverend Fred Shuttlesworth, one of the founding members of the SCLC, asked the group to turn its attention next to Birmingham, Alabama. The city had been nicknamed Bombingham because segregationists bombed so many of its churches and homes. The SCLC developed a clear plan of action, with the goal of desegregating the downtown business district.

Theophilus Eugene "Bull" Connor, the commissioner of public safety, ruled Birmingham with an iron fist. Whites were as afraid of him as African Americans were. He did not hesitate to attack demonstrators, whether children or adults, with police dogs, fire hoses, and billy clubs.

During the demonstrations, Dr. King—who was, by now, a well-known national figure—was arrested, just as he hoped. King wanted to focus the media's attention on Conner, so that the public would learn of his behavior and pressure the government to take action. The SCLC's James Bevel had the idea to include a march of schoolchildren as part of the protest. Reporters and photographers were there watching when Conner used his brutal tactics on the children. The news and images shocked the world—and all eyes were suddenly on Birmingham.

While King was serving his nine days in jail, he received a letter from a group of white clergy who criticized the demonstrations. King's twenty-page response, "Letter from a Birmingham Jail," is the most famous of all his writings. On May 10, 1963, Alabama businessmen agreed to desegregate downtown Montgomery.

On June 19, 1963, President John F. Kennedy delivered a new, stronger civil rights bill to Congress for approval. Dr. King, the SCLC, and all the other civil rights organizations decided to join together to make sure that the bill would become law. They organized a massive demonstration to show the public's support of a new law protecting civil rights.

The March on Washington for Jobs and Freedom took place on August 28, 1963. On that peaceful day of demonstration, about 250,000 to 400,000 people of all races came together to show their support for equality and justice. King closed the historic event with his famous "I Have a Dream" speech, which he delivered in front of the Lincoln Memorial.

The Civil Rights Act was signed into law on July 2, 1964. That year, at age thirty-five, Dr. King became the first African American to be named *Time* magazine's Man of the Year. In October, while King lay in a hospital bed recovering from fatigue, he learned that he had been awarded the 1964 Nobel Peace Prize.

King knew that prizes did not bring freedom. He turned his energy to voting rights. Throughout the South, African Americans were being blocked from freely exercising their right to vote. King decided to focus national attention on Selma, Alabama. On March 7, 1965, protesters planned to march from Selma to the state capitol in Montgomery. Student leader John Lewis and Hosea Williams of the SCLC led the march. King planned to join them on the road.

Two hundred state police and sheriff's deputies blocked the six hundred marchers on their way out of Selma on the Edmund Pettus Bridge. The protesters were ordered to turn around and go back. Hosea Williams asked if the group could have a moment to pray. The marchers knelt on the bridge, and the police began to attack them. The violent incident became known as Bloody Sunday. Once again, television and newspaper cameras recorded the scene for the nation and the world to see.

King, who was in Atlanta, received word of the attack and immediately sent out telegrams to high-ranking clergy across the nation. "In the vicious maltreatment of defenseless citizens of Selma, where old women and young children were gassed and clubbed at random, we have witnessed an eruption of the disease of racism which seeks to destroy all America," he wrote. "Join me in Selma for a ministers' march to Montgomery on Tuesday morning, March 9."

King led some six hundred blacks and whites on a fifty-mile trek from Selma to the state capitol in Montgomery. By the time they reached the city, the number of marchers had swelled to twenty-five thousand. On August 6, 1965, President Lyndon Johnson signed the Voting Rights Act, which President Kennedy had submitted to Congress the year before.

That same year, U.S. involvement in the war in Vietnam was escalating, and the civil rights of Americans were no longer the nation's main concern. King opposed the Vietnam War, which isolated him from some of his friends in government. His position on civil rights was also under attack by some African Americans, such as Stokely Carmichael and others, who believed in more militant forms of protest. The civil rights movement crumbled around King, along with the movement's commitment to nonviolence as a means for social change.

On April 4, 1968, Dr. King was shot and killed on the balcony outside his room at the Lorraine Motel in Memphis, Tennessee. James Earl Ray was arrested and sentenced to life for the murder. The motel where the leader was killed is today the National Civil Rights Museum.

In 1968, Coretta Scott King established the Martin Luther King Jr. Center for Non-Violent Social Change, in Atlanta, Georgia. The King Center's Freedom Hall Complex is the first institution of its kind built to honor an African American. It includes the King Center, King's tomb, and a twenty-three-acre park that includes King's childhood home and the Ebenezer

Baptist Church, where he and his father preached. Committed to maintaining a living history of the civil rights movement, Mrs. King preserved her husband's papers. The King Center Library and Archives boasts the most extensive collection of documents from the civil rights era.

Since 1986, Martin Luther King Day has been a national holiday. Every January, Americans participate in educational programs, exhibitions, and parades in his honor. As the leader of the American civil rights movement, King changed the country forever, and his words and deeds will continue to inspire and shape future generations.

DOROTHY FOREMAN COTTON

CIVIL RIGHTS LEADER, EDUCATOR

(c. 1931–)

*Because of my work in the civil rights movement, I see the humanity
and the divinity, the capacity in people that I did not see before.
I know that they, too, are lights on the planet.*

Dorothy Foreman Cotton was one of the most important women in the life of Dr. Martin Luther King Jr. She was born in Goldsboro, North Carolina. Her mother died when she was only three years of age. Her father, Claude Foreman, worked in a tobacco factory and raised his four daughters alone.

Cotton's high school English teacher, Rosa Gray, knew the family's situation and saw the young girl's talent. She arranged for Dorothy to attend North Carolina's historically black Shaw University. She also arranged for her to work as a housekeeper for the university's president. When her employer took a new job as president of Virginia State College, in Petersburg, Virginia, Cotton transferred to the college and completed her degree in English and library science there. She then went to Boston University to earn her graduate degree in special education.

When Cotton returned to Petersburg in 1960, the civil rights movement was in full swing. She joined her minister, the Reverend Wyatt T. Walker, who was also the leader of the local National Association for the Advancement of Colored People (NAACP). They protested in picket lines in front of the local Woolworth's department store and the public library, both of which banned African Americans from entering.

Cotton first met Dr. King when he was invited to speak at a meeting in Petersburg. Afterward, they both had supper at Walker's home. "I remember Martin Luther King as very unimpressive, very unassuming, just sitting there at the end of the table," she said. "Only later did I realize his powerful personal presence." When King offered Walker the position of executive director of the Southern Christian Leadership Conference (SCLC), Walker said he would accept only if Cotton could accompany him to work in the Atlanta, Georgia, headquarters.

Cotton is sometimes wrongly described as Dr. King's secretary. In fact, from 1960 to 1972, she was the education director for the SCLC. She was the only female member of the executive staff of the organization.

Cotton's job was the day-to-day management of the Citizenship Education Program. The SCLC had inherited this progressive program from the Highlander Folk School. She was responsible for developing educational programs for local leadership and teaching nonviolent strategies for creating social change. Cotton worked with civil rights activists Septima Poinsette Clark, Bernice Robinson, and Andrew Young. "The people who came to SCLC's leadership training program were ready to be engaged in activities that would better their lives," Cotton said. "Essentially, we helped people from all over the South to discover the capacities they had within, capacities that helped them solve the problems facing their communities."

Cotton was a key participant in all the major events of the civil rights movement. She became one of King's closest confidantes and an important member of his inner circle. When King was assassinated in 1968, Cotton was devastated. "I was in mourning for two or three years," she said. "We all were. I still miss his physical presence and his friendship."

After King's death, Cotton continued to work for the SCLC, now under the leadership of Rev. Ralph Abernathy. In 1978, she became the southeastern regional director for ACTION, a federal agency for volunteer programs. For a short period, she also served as vice president of field operations for the Martin Luther King Jr. Center for Non-Violent Social Change, in Atlanta, Georgia. For nine years, she was director of student activities at Cornell University in Ithaca, New York.

Cotton now travels throughout the world as a lecturer and motivational speaker. She conducts seminars on leadership, individual empowerment, and social change. In her presentations, she often tells the story of the civil rights movement through the inspiring Freedom Songs of the era.

She is also one of the founders of the National Citizenship School, which teaches people how to create institutions that support individual growth and development. She has received honorary degrees from the University of New England and from Spelman College in Atlanta. "I cannot change the whole world," she once said. "But the lesson I took from the sixties, and hold to now, is that we can change the parts of it that we touch."

RICHARD "DICK" CLAXTON GREGORY

COMEDIAN, CIVIL RIGHTS ACTIVIST, AUTHOR
(1932–)

The last time I was down South I walked into this restaurant, and this white waitress came up to me and said, "We don't serve colored people." I said, "That's all right, I don't eat colored people. Bring me a whole fried chicken."

Dick Gregory was born in St. Louis, Missouri, on October 12,1932. By age nine, he was working shining shoes in a "whites only" bar in St Louis. "One day I was cleaning this lady's shoes," he remembered. "When you're putting the sole dressing on, you have to put your hand behind the heel, to steady it. I heard this man say: 'Take your hand off that white woman's leg, boy.' Then he kicked me in the mouth and broke my front teeth. The owner threw me out and told me not to come back."

In high school, Gregory was a celebrated track star. He attended Southern Illinois University on a track scholarship. He was the first African American in eighty-four years to win the school's Outstanding Athlete Award. Gregory had to leave school in 1954, when he was drafted into the U.S. Army. During his time in the military, he discovered that he could make people laugh. His comedy routines won him first place in several talent shows and a chance to entertain the troops and tour with Special Services.

In 1956, after he was discharged from the army, Gregory returned to the university, but soon he left again. He no longer believed that a college education would prevent racial discrimination and lead to better job opportunities. He set out to begin his career as a comedian.

In 1961, his agent booked him at a club in Chicago, Illinois. When Gregory arrived to perform, the manager informed him that the clients were executives from the South and, because of the South's racist views toward blacks, they might not be a good audience. Because Gregory had run twenty blocks to get to the club and did not have money for transportation home, he took the stage. He withstood the crowd's insults and hecklers with his quick comebacks. At the end of an hourlong routine, he received a standing ovation and tips from the Southern patrons.

Gregory continued to push the limits of his racially charged humor. When Chicago's famous Playboy Club hired him to perform there for more than three years, he quickly became a national celebrity.

In 1962, Gregory decided to travel south to work for civil rights. The state of Mississippi had refused to distribute federal food supplies to areas that held voter registration drives for African Americans. So Gregory chartered a plane and delivered several tons of food himself. In 1963, he suffered what he called the worst beating of his life, following a march against school segregation in Birmingham. He later recalled, "After we'd been arrested, I saw this officer trying to pull a little boy out of our cell. I tried to stop him because I was afraid what he might do. So many people disappeared. They beat me with baseball bats."

The same year, his autobiography, *Nigger,* was the number-one book on the best-seller list. In the beginning of the book, he explains the controversial title in a note to his mother: "When we're through, Momma, there won't be any niggers anymore. . . . Wherever you are, if you ever hear the word 'nigger' again, remember they are advertising my book." To date, more than seven million copies have been sold.

In 1968, Gregory ran for president of the United States as a member of the Freedom and Peace Party. He received more than 1.5 million votes in his challenge against Republican nominee Richard Nixon and Democratic nominee Hubert Humphrey.

The comedian-activist and his wife, Lil, were arrested and jailed more than fifty times. He once watched a Mississippi sheriff kick Lil, who was nine months pregnant at the time. "I had to convince myself that the reason I did nothing was that I was nonviolent," he said, but he realized the real reason he did nothing was because he was afraid. "But afterwards I decided that if I wouldn't hit a man who kicked my pregnant wife, I couldn't participate in the destruction of any animal that never harmed me."

Gregory became a vegetarian and turned his new lifestyle into a weapon against racism. He fasted to protest world hunger and went on a liquid diet for more than two years to protest the war in Vietnam. Gregory has fasted more than sixty times as a nonviolent action against injustice.

In 1992, he established the Campaign for Human Dignity to fight crime in troubled areas in his hometown of St. Louis. In 1996, the national media made public charges that the Central Intelligence Agency (CIA) had supplied cocaine to largely African American neighborhoods in Los Angeles, California, to give rise to the crack epidemic. Gregory was among the first to protest at CIA headquarters, where he was arrested.

In addition to producing numerous comedy albums, Gregory has published several books, including *Callus on My Soul: A Memoir,* which was

Dick Gregory (second from left) participates in a protest against segregation in public schools.

released in 2003. Today, Gregory remains dedicated to his role as an activist. "This is a revolution," he said. "It started long before I came into it, and I may die before it's over, but we'll bust this thing and cut out this cancer. America will be as strong and beautiful as it should be, for black folks and white folks."

ANDREW JACKSON YOUNG JR.

CIVIL RIGHTS LEADER

(1932–)

In a world where change is inevitable and continuous, the need to achieve that change without violence is essential for survival.

Andrew Young was born in New Orleans, Louisiana, on March 12, 1932. His father was a successful dentist who expected his son to attend dental school and one day join him in his thriving practice. Andrew attended private schools for the black elite of New Orleans society.

When Young graduated from Howard University in Washington, D.C., he did not know what he wanted to do with his life—but he knew he did not want to become a dentist. In 1951, he found his answer at a youth conference sponsored by the United Church of Christ (UCC) in Lake Brownwood, Texas. Young was one of only two African Americans attending. At that time, the South was segregated, and blacks did not usually interact socially with whites.

The young people's commitment to church service so impressed Young that he decided he would devote his life to the ministry, too. "I had never before met any white people whose personal faith made a difference in their actions on the question of race," he said. "This experience made me examine my own faith. It also led me to seminary." Young entered Hartford Divinity School in Hartford, Connecticut, and received his degree in divinity in 1955. He was ordained as a minister of the United Church of Christ (UCC).

Young served a congregation in Thomasville, Georgia. While there, he led a voter registration drive. This experience gave him his first taste of civil rights activism—and it wasn't his last. In 1957, at age twenty-five, the leaders of the National Council of Churches (NCC) asked Young to work as ambassador for the Youth Division of Christian Education. He held the position for three years.

Young's work for the NCC changed his way of seeing the world. "I saw that our government was ruled by our fears of Communism rather than wisdom and understanding about the world in which we live," he said. He also began to view the members of other freedom movements—in Africa, Latin America, and the Middle East—as brothers, all working for the same goals.

In 1961, Young became involved with the Southern Christian Leadership Conference (SCLC), which was headed by Dr. Martin Luther King Jr. and Ella Baker. Young joined the SCLC's Citizenship Education Program in Atlanta, Georgia. He helped raised funds through his contacts and influence in the UCC.

The SCLC's program taught black citizens how to read and interpret the U.S. Constitution. In the South, African Americans had to take strict tests before they could register to vote. Any person who did not pass the test could not vote in an election. Young also trained civil rights activists in nonviolent protest tactics, which were an essential part of the movement. Within a few months, Young became a member of Dr. King's trusted inner circle.

Whenever the SCLC staged a demonstration, Young was sent in to present the protesters' demands to the government officials. Although these demands might appear reasonable to us today, at the time they were controversial. Civil rights activists demanded that blacks simply have the right to eat in restaurants, sit wherever they like on a bus, and work as salesclerks. Before the civil rights movement changed the South, blacks were not allowed to eat with whites or sit near whites on a bus. They could not hold jobs other than those in food or janitorial services.

In 1972, Young became the first black U.S. representative from the state of Georgia since 1870. He served in Congress for three terms. In 1977, President Jimmy Carter appointed him as U.S. ambassador to the United Nations. Young also was elected to two terms as the mayor of Atlanta in 1981 and 1985. The Andrew Young School of Policy Studies at Georgia State University is one of the country's best schools in the field.

Today, Rev. Young is on the board of the Martin Luther King Jr. Center for Non-Violent Social Change in Atlanta. He believes that racism is a "symptom of poverty" and often speaks to raise awareness of the issue of poverty in America. "Most of the problems we face in America, whether crime or education problems or hate groups," he said, "are derived from what Martin Luther King used to call 'the lonely islands of poverty in the midst of this ocean of material wealth.'"

UNITA BLACKWELL

CIVIL RIGHTS LEADER, MISSISSIPPI

(1933–)

*I guess I was born in it, I was born in the movement;
the day I was born I was born black.*

Unita Blackwell was born March 18,
1933, in Lula, Mississippi. Along
the Mississippi Delta, the living
conditions were bad for African Americans.
Her mother and family were hardworking
sharecroppers, but their earnings from
picking cotton were barely enough to
survive. The state of Mississippi had no
interest in educating African American
children. Unita had to attend school
in nearby West Helena, Arkansas. Her
education did not save her from the cotton
fields and the abusive sharecropping system.
She picked cotton well into her adult years.

Blackwell heard about the Freedom
Rides and the rumors that civil rights

workers were making their way to Mississippi. One Sunday morning, a representative from the Student Nonviolent Coordinating Committee (SNCC) spoke at a local church. There in Issaquena County—and elsewhere throughout the South—African Americans who tried to register to vote were beaten, put in jail, and sometimes murdered. The SNCC representative asked for volunteers who had the courage to go down to the county courthouse to register. "And I stood up," Blackwell said. "My husband caught me by the dress tail and pulled me back down, because he was supposed to stand up first, you see, because he's the man. So he stood, then I stood up, and I've been standing up ever since."

The day that she went to the county registrar's office, an angry mob of whites harassed her and the other volunteers who were with her. Blackwell was not allowed to register and returned home unharmed. Because she had tried to vote, however, she lost her job picking cotton and could no longer get work cleaning houses. She began working as a field worker for the SNCC.

In 1964, African Americans represented 45 percent of the population of Mississippi, but only 5 percent were registered to vote. SNCC members wanted to educate and register African Americans by the end of the summer, before the 1964 elections. When that summer—called Freedom Summer— began, Blackwell was appointed SNCC's summer project director for Issaquena County.

Blackwell was a target for angry whites. She was arrested every day for thirty days in a row. "They would just take you to jail, and you'd pay your way out for twelve fifty. Somebody would try to scrape up the money." So many Molotov cocktails were thrown in Blackwell's front yard, she had to teach her son how to identify the explosive device and warned him not to touch them.

Freedom Summer provided Blackwell, a woman from one of the poorest communities in the United States, with the opportunity to discover her own power as a leader. Freedom Summer changed the way she saw herself and

Members of the Mississippi Freedom Democratic Party

the world. She once said, "All my life I knew something was wrong with the way that people perceived me as a black person, 'cause I was born in the Mississippi Delta."

Blackwell opened her two-bedroom house to middle-class, white youth who would sleep on the floor and work to register voters under her direction. She worked with Fannie Lou Hamer to found the Mississippi Freedom Democratic Party (MFDP), which challenged the all-white Mississippi delegation at the 1964 Democratic National Convention.

In 1966, President Lyndon B. Johnson declared a war on poverty. The needs of the poor in the Mississippi Delta were not addressed in his plan, however. So in January of that year, Blackwell, nine other activists, and about forty citizens took over the U.S. Air Force Base in Greenville, Mississippi. They demanded that the federal government provide them with food, land, job training, and jobs. Blackwell was the group's key spokesperson.

The focus of the civil rights movement shifted to women's rights. During the late 1960s and early 1970s, Blackwell served as a community development specialist with the National Council of Negro Women. In 1976, she was the first African American woman to be elected mayor in the state of Mississippi. As mayor, she brought running water, a sewage system, and paved roads to the town of Mayersville. She has continually been reelected and still serves as mayor of the much-improved town.

In 1979, Blackwell participated in President Jimmy Carter's Energy Summit at Camp David. She later earned a master's degree in regional planning from the University of Massachusetts–Amherst. In 1992, she received a prestigious MacArthur Foundation Fellowship, which is also sometimes called a "genius grant."

Blackwell's passion for civil rights and human rights has led her to Africa and Asia to learn about the challenges people in those places face. She has also served as president of the U.S.-China Peoples Friendship Association and has visited China several times to help open dialogue between the two countries. She believes that "the same principle applies to international relations as to relations within countries. It's all about understanding and working together to forge solutions."

WALTER FAUNTROY

CIVIL RIGHTS ACTIVIST AND LOBBYIST

(1933–)

I learned everything I needed to know about life in that Sunday school.

Nine-year-old Walter Fauntroy loved to attend the children's program at New Bethel Baptist Church in Washington, D.C. He became a member of the church in 1942, when the Sunday school teacher, Harriet Epps, combed the neighborhood looking for boys and girls to attend her classes. Little did she know that Fauntroy would grow up to become the minister of New Bethel Baptist Church and a leader in the civil rights movement.

Walter Fauntroy was born February 6, 1933. His father told stories of his struggles against racism and how he had "lifted two generations of white people over his shoulders to be his supervisors" at work. Fauntroy said that he "heard at the dinner

Walter Fauntroy, Bayard Rustin, and Julius Hobson meet with police chief Robert V. Murray to discuss a civil rights rally planned for August 28, 1963 (from left: Murray, Fauntroy, Rustin, Hobson).

table about the way white people treat us [blacks] and deny us five things: income, education, health care, housing, and justice."

Two years after Fauntroy joined New Bethel, he decided to become a minister. His first sermon, at the age of seventeen, inspired the congregation to support his calling. Church members sold chitlins, fish, and chicken dinners to help pay for his college tuition.

Fauntroy attended Virginia Union University, which is where he first met Martin Luther King Jr. King was on his way to Boston University to begin his doctoral studies and needed a place to stay, so Fauntroy shared his room. The two men talked all night about the peaceful teachings of the Indian leader Mohandas Gandhi and how they could fight racism in America. In 1955, Fauntroy graduated from Virginia Union with a degree in history. He then won a scholarship to Yale University Divinity School, where he completed his bachelor of divinity degree in 1958.

Fauntroy's understanding of the Gospels led him to become a politician. Inspired by an Old Testament verse from the book of Isaiah, Fauntroy made it his life's mission to "declare good news to the poor." He believed the purpose of politics was to provide for the people most in need. He also believed that it was his duty as a Christian "not simply to talk that talk on Sunday—to sing it up from the choir, preach it up from the pulpit, or shout it up from the pews—but when it's over, to do something to provide for 'the least of these!'"

The proud Yale graduate returned to New Bethel Church in 1958. The church's longtime pastor had died, and the members wanted Fauntroy to take his place. During the next few months, the civil rights movement gained momentum. Dr. Martin Luther King Jr. was now president of the Southern Christian Leadership Conference (SCLC). King knew that his friend shared his views on social change. He asked Fauntroy to work for civil rights as SCLC's lead lobbyist on Capitol Hill in Washington, D.C. Fauntroy was soon named president of the SCLC's Washington bureau.

Fauntroy, a talented strategist, planned many of the major protests of the civil rights movement. He organized the 1961 Freedom Rides on buses throughout the South and the historic 1963 March on Washington, which brought hundreds of thousands of protesters to the Washington Monument. He also coordinated James Meredith's 1964 March Against Fear, the 1965 march from Selma to Montgomery, Alabama, and countless sit-ins and demonstrations.

In 1966, President Lyndon B. Johnson asked Fauntroy to help chair the To Fulfill These Rights conference, where black and white leaders gathered to discuss ways to provide equality and opportunity for black Americans. Fauntroy was also a key player in the passage of the 1964 Civil Rights Act and the 1965 Voting Rights Act.

Fauntroy stayed true to his mission to help the poor. In 1969, after the assassination of Dr. King, Fauntroy organized the Poor People's Campaign in

King's honor. His Model Inner City Community Organization, created to restore his run-down neighborhood, won the attention of the president. Johnson appointed Fauntroy to act as vice-chair of Washington's first city council.

In 1970, Fauntroy became the first elected D.C. delegate to Congress. The next year, the Congressional Black Caucus (CBC) was established to positively influence the lives of African Americans through domestic and international programs. Fauntroy was among the CBC's founding members.

Fauntroy proudly served in Congress for ten terms and worked his way up through the ranks to chair several committees. He also founded the National Black Leadership Roundtable. The Roundtable is a group of the top members of 250 major organizations, including the National Association for the Advancement of Colored People (NAACP), the National Urban League, and the Leadership Conference on Civil Rights.

In 1984, when the U.S. government refused to take a stand against apartheid in South Africa, Fauntroy and three other civil rights activists met with the South African ambassador. They listened as the ambassador spoke about "how wonderful apartheid was and how the blacks loved it." The activists informed the ambassador that they would remain in his office until the policy was abolished. The four were arrested, but their action set off protests throughout the country.

Fauntroy retired from Congress in 1990, but not from his career as an advocate for civil rights. Today, he is still delivering "good news" to his congregation at New Bethel Baptist Church.

JAMES MEREDITH

CIVIL RIGHTS ACTIVIST, MISSISSIPPI

(1933–)

I have always been a "conscientious objector" to my "oppressed status" as long as I can remember. My long-cherished ambition has been to break the monopoly on rights and privileges held by the whites of the state of Mississippi.

James Meredith was born in Attala, Mississippi, on June 25, 1933. The seventh of thirteen children, Meredith walked 4 miles (6.4 km) to school each day. There was no bus for African American children, so he—like most African American children in the South—watched the all-white school bus pass by every morning.

During his senior year of high school, Meredith won an essay contest. The assignment was to explain "why I am so proud to be an American." He wrote that he was proud of the American ideal that "an individual has the right to grow and develop according to his ability and ingenuity, and is not restricted from progress solely on the basis of his race." He set out to make America live up to that promise.

After nine years in the U.S. Air Force, Meredith enrolled in Jackson State University, a historically black college. During his tour of duty, he had attended night school at four different colleges and had completed courses at the University of Maryland's overseas program. So when he entered Jackson State, he had to take only a little more than a year's worth of classes in order to graduate. Meredith decided not to finish his degree at Jackson State, however. He wanted to graduate from the all-white University of Mississippi in Oxford, which was popularly known as Ole Miss.

Meredith had applied to Ole Miss before, but even though he was a good student, he never received a response. This time, he asked for help. He talked with Medgar Evers, Mississippi field secretary for the National Association for the Advancement of Colored People (NAACP). Evers suggested Meredith contact Thurgood Marshall, head of the NAACP Legal Defense and Educational Fund.

In 1961, a few days before he applied for the spring semester at Ole Miss, Meredith wrote Marshall a letter. If he had legal help from the NAACP, Meredith knew that he could break the racial barriers at colleges and universities throughout the South. "I am making this move in what I consider the interest of and for the benefit of: (1) my country, (2) my race, (3) my family, and (4) myself," he wrote. A week later, Meredith was refused admission to Ole Miss, and the court case began.

Thurgood Marshall turned over the case to his trusted colleague, Constance Baker Motley. In September 1962, a federal court ordered Ole Miss to admit Meredith. Many whites were outraged by the court's decision. Mississippi's governor, Ross Barnett, a man described by *Time* magazine as "the most bitter racist in the nation," said, "We must either submit to the unlawful dictate of the federal government or stand up like men and

James Meredith walks across the University of Mississippi campus.

tell them, Never." President John F. Kennedy had to send U.S. marshals to Oxford to ensure Meredith's safety on his first day of school.

Riots broke out on September 29, 1962, and thirty-five thousand U.S. troops arrived in Oxford. Amid tear gas, the crowd was in hand-to-hand combat for fourteen hours. "I was more frightened in Mississippi than I was at Pearl Harbor or anytime during the war," one U.S. marshal reported. When it was finally over, almost four hundred people were injured, two killed, and two hundred arrested. The following morning, Meredith registered for classes in peace. In a later interview, he shared a memorable experience as he headed for his first class:

> *There was a black standing in the hall, and I know that looked a little strange, and he had a broom under his arm so the broom handle would touch me and he was delivering one . . . message that I got at Ole Miss. The message was that we're looking after you—every black eye, looking after you. And the look on his face, that was a greater act of defiance than what I was doing because he could have lost his job.*

In 1963, Meredith graduated from the University of Mississippi with a degree in political science. At his graduation, he wore a button that white segregationists had handed out the year before during their protest against him. The button said "Never." Meredith pinned the button to his robe upside down as a sign of victory.

By 1966, Meredith was a law student at Columbia University in New York, but the hate and violence that blacks had to endure in the South was still uppermost on his mind. On June 5, he set out by himself on what he called a March Against Fear to encourage African Americans to confront the terrible fear that paralyzed so many of them. Meredith began his march in Memphis, Tennessee, and planned to continue to Jackson, Mississippi. Shortly after he set out, however, he was shot and wounded by sniper fire. When word got out that Meredith had been injured, many civil rights leaders—including Dr. Martin Luther King Jr., Stokely Carmichael, and Floyd McKissick—continued the march in Meredith's honor.

"I think that the greatest tribute that we can pay him [Meredith] as he lies on his sickbed as a result of being shot yesterday, is to go out and work harder to remove the conditions from our society and from the state of Mississippi that made it possible for him to be shot," King said in a speech he delivered during the march.

Fed and nourished by locals along the way, an estimated two thousand people joined the march to Jackson. More than three thousand African Americans registered to vote during the march. Meredith rejoined the march on June 24 and attended the rally of fifteen thousand people that welcomed the marchers at the state capitol in Jackson on June 26.

Deeply troubled by the shooting in 1966, Meredith eventually distanced himself from the movement. Civil rights leaders believed Meredith's actions built support for the Civil Rights Act of 1964 and helped many other African Americans break the long-held racial barriers of the South.

MYRLIE EVERS-WILLIAMS

CIVIL RIGHTS LEADER

(1933–)

*I believe the future of this country lies in our ability
to work together as a people to create a truly just society.*

Myrlie Evers-Williams, the widow of civil rights martyr Medgar Evers, is one of the most extraordinary African American women in history. She was born Myrlie Beasley on June 12, 1933, in Vicksburg, Mississippi. She was raised by two schoolteachers—her grandmother, Annie McCain Beasley, and her aunt, Myrlie Beasley Polk—and they made sure Williams attended college.

In 1950, thousands of African American veterans of World War II were attending college with the help of the G.I. Bill of Rights. As she gave Myrlie a final hug good-bye, Annie Beasley warned her young granddaughter not to get involved with "those veterans."

Myrlie met war veteran Medgar Evers in the "first hour of [her] first day" at Alcorn State Agricultural and Mechanical College. They fell in love, and eighteen-year-old Myrlie left school the next year to marry Evers on Christmas Eve. Evers was a civil rights activist and field secretary for the National Association for the Advancement of Colored People (NAACP). Myrlie helped him run his Jackson, Mississippi, office. Together they organized voter registration drives, sit-ins, and rallies. She described her husband as "a man who liked to rock the boat." "Medgar knew what he was doing," she said, "and he knew what the risks were. He just decided that he had to do what he had to do. But I knew at some point in time that he would be taken from me."

In June 1960, Evers was gunned down in front of the couple's home by white supremacist Byron De La Beckwith. With her Southern grace and strength, but no income, Myrlie began to rebuild her life without her husband.

As Evers's widow, she was in high demand as a public speaker, and her presentations raised money for the NAACP. Contributions to the organization reached the highest levels in history. There was also was a dramatic increase in membership. Finally, Myrlie convinced the NAACP's national secretary, Roy Wilkins, to pay her Evers's salary in exchange for her work for the organization. The small income was enough to allow her to support her three children while she returned to college to finish her degree.

Myrlie and her children moved to California. She graduated from Pomona College in Claremont and then relocated to Los Angeles. She was active in the political community and was one of few women to run for Congress in 1969. In 1975, she married Walter Williams, a longshoreman and union organizer. In June 1988, Mayor Tom Bradley made Myrlie the first black woman appointed to Los Angeles's five-member board of public works. She managed a budget of nearly one billion dollars and a staff of five thousand employees.

Although he had been tried twice, Medgar Evers's assassin was never convicted of the crime. Myrlie wanted De La Beckwith to pay for his crime, and she visited Mississippi regularly to "keep tabs" on him and to search for witnesses and evidence. She learned about an organization called the Mississippi Sovereignty Commission, which spied on civil rights activists and groups and had withheld evidence in the case.

In 1994, Myrlie—with the help and support of committed journalist Jerry Mitchell—convinced the district attorney in Jackson to reopen the case. This time, with a jury that—for the first time—included African Americans, Byron De La Beckwith was found guilty and sentenced to life in prison. "Medgar's life was not in vain, and perhaps he did more in death than he could have in life. Somehow I think he is still among us," Myrlie said.

In 1995, her husband of twenty years, Walter Williams, died of cancer. Myrlie continued to make history. She was the first woman to become chairman of the board of the NAACP. She is the co-author of *For Us, the Living*, a book about Medgar Evers and the civil rights movement, which was adapted as a television movie. Her second book was an autobiography entitled *Watch Me Fly: What I Learned on the Way to Becoming the Woman I Was Meant to Be.*

After her retirement from the NAACP, Myrlie established the Medgar Evers Institute in Jackson, Mississippi. The institute promotes racial and ethnic relations in America and creates leadership programs for youth. In her autobiography, Myrlie describes this later phase of her life as "an opportunity to fully be who I am: a woman hell bent on slowing down and equally determined to continue to make a difference in the world."

ROBERT "BOB" MOSES

CIVIL RIGHTS ACTIVIST, ORGANIZER, AND EDUCATOR

(1935–)

The demands of a high-tech age make math literacy as much an issue today as voting was in the Jim Crow South half a century ago.

Robert Moses was born in Harlem, New York, on January 23, 1935. His family was poor, but because he did so well in grade school, he had opportunities that were not available to many of the other people he knew. Moses was able to attend a private high school and earn a graduate and doctoral degree from Harvard University.

While visiting an uncle in Newport News, Virginia, Moses participated in a sit-in. He had heard about nonviolent protests as a means to change society, but now that he had experienced one, he understood how powerful they could be. He believed nonviolent protest could help improve conditions for African Americans and the poor.

In 1960, Moses joined the Student Nonviolent Coordinating Committee (SNCC) and moved to Atlanta, Georgia. He worked closely with Ella Baker, who was an adviser to the SNCC and also the executive director of the Southern Christian Leadership Conference (SCLC). Baker wanted to organize an SNCC conference in Atlanta for those students in the South who were working for civil rights, but she did not know how to find them. She sent Moses to find them.

Baker pointed Moses to Cleveland, Mississippi, where he met Amzie Moore. Moore was a farmer and also chairman of the local chapter of the National Association for the Advancement of Colored People (NAACP). Moore and Moses became friends.

In 1963, the two men began work on a project called the Freedom Vote. The project was organized by the Council of Federated Organizations (COFO), which included all the large civil rights organizations working in Mississippi. Moses was one of the directors of COFO. The goal of the project was to prove to politicians that black citizens wanted to vote and also to teach blacks—many of whom had never voted before—how to cast a ballot.

Moses and Moore worked on this dangerous but important project for four years. Moses later said, "The story of the voter registration drive in the South in the decade of the 1960s is a story of people struggling for greater control over the decision making that affects their lives, of people who learn to step forward to make a demand on society in their own voices."

Blacks in Mississippi lived in the rich, fertile, cotton-growing land of the Delta, but they lived on plantations controlled by wealthy landowners. Without the power to vote, they had no say in local politics—which meant they had no control over the educational system or other matters that affected their lives. If African Americans could vote, they could change their conditions. The landowners and others did not want the situation to change, however, so they did everything they could to keep blacks from voting.

Bob Moses teaches an algebra class in 1999.

During this period, a wave of terror was sweeping through Mississippi. Churches and homes across the state were firebombed to scare blacks into abandoning their efforts to integrate schools and claim their voting rights. Mississippians and SNCC volunteers were murdered as a warning to others. In 1963, more than ninety thousand black citizens of Mississippi voted in the Freedom Vote mock election.

Today, Moses lives in Cambridge, Massachusetts. He has developed a program called the Algebra Project, which helps children improve their math skills. He says that computers, the "tools that control the technology," are based on the mathematical language of algebra. He believes that by learning this language, children of color will gain a powerful advantage in the computer-driven world of tomorrow.

Moses believes that education is the key to opportunity and that it gives people the freedom and power to control their own lives. He has said, "What is central now is the need for economic access; the political process has been opened—there are no formal barriers to voting, for example—but economic access, taking advantage of new technologies and economic opportunity, demands as much effort as political struggle required in the 1960s."

MARION SHEPILOV BARRY JR.

CIVIL RIGHTS LEADER, POLITICIAN

(1936–)

It was like a war. You change your tactics depending on where you are on the battlefield. I was definitely on the outer edges of society in terms of some of the programs I was moving. And society has always needed pressure to bring about basic changes.

Marion Shepilov Barry Jr. was born in Itta Bena, Mississippi, the son of a sharecropper family. When Barry was eight years old, he and his mother and sister moved from the plantation to the city of Memphis, Tennessee.

As a child, Barry was always busy and never shied away from hard work. He picked cotton with his mother, worked as a paperboy and as a waiter, and volunteered for church work. He was one of the first black Eagle Scouts of the Boy Scouts of America in the state of Tennessee. He was also a straight-A student at Booker T. Washington High School and played football and basketball. His high energy was a great asset to him throughout his life.

Barry attended LeMoyne College, a historically black school (now LeMoyne-Owen College) in Memphis, on an academic scholarship. In his senior year, he read a newspaper article about racist statements made by Walter Chandler, a member of the university's board of trustees. Barry was then the president of the university's chapter of the National Association for the Advancement of Colored People (NAACP). He convinced three members of the NAACP to join him in writing a letter calling for Chandler to resign or be removed from the board.

The letter caused a stir in the school and in the local community. The board of trustees pressured the school to punish Barry. Two weeks before graduation, the college threatened to kick him out. "The president told me he was going to expel me and I said, 'I don't think so,'" Barry said later. "Luckily, for me, the community came out in support of me and I was allowed to graduate."

Barry learned that by working to help the community, he had gained a solid reputation and a base of support. This support gave him the power to challenge those in authority and to make needed changes in unfair systems. He would remember that lesson later, when he was serving as mayor of Washington, D.C.

After graduating in 1958, Barry enrolled in graduate school at Fisk University in Nashville. While at Fisk, he participated in the Reverend James Lawson's training sessions through the Nashville chapter of the Southern Christian Leadership Conference (SCLC). Lawson was training SCLC members in methods of nonviolent protest.

In 1960, Barry, Diane Nash, John Lewis, Rev. C. T. Vivian, Rev. James Bevel, and James Forman were at the center of a student-led sit-in campaign to desegregate restaurants in downtown Nashville. From February through May, the protesters were repeatedly taunted, beaten, arrested, and jailed for attempting to sit at "whites only" lunch counters.

The sit-in protests eventually succeeded. After being confronted by the protesters, the city's mayor publicly admitted that discrimination based on race and skin color was immoral and unacceptable. On May 10, 1960, the downtown restaurants of Nashville were opened to blacks and whites.

The sit-in movement swept through the South like wildfire. Students everywhere staged sit-ins to protest the segregation of schools, parks, restaurants, swimming pools, movie theaters, and other public places. With the help of Ella Baker, the executive director of the SCLC, the students named their organization the Student Nonviolent Coordinating Committee (SNCC). Barry was elected as its first chairman.

From 1960 through 1964, Barry traveled through the South organizing voter registrations and sit-ins. It was dangerous work. White segregationists were often violent. Many students were beaten and others were killed. The difficulties and hardships only made Barry more determined to keep fighting.

During this time, Barry enrolled in a doctoral program in chemistry at the University of Tennessee, but he gave it up after three years. He decided instead to devote all of his energy to the civil rights movement. In 1965, he moved to Washington, D.C., to organize a new SNCC chapter. In 1967, he cofounded Pride Inc., a nonprofit organization that employed more than one thousand high school dropouts and convicts who were unable to find jobs. Pride Inc. also tried to help support new, small businesses in low-income areas. Barry was a constant presence in the neighborhood streets of Washington, talking to people and encouraging them.

Barry realized that, in the next phase of the civil rights movement, blacks had to become involved in politics. The time for "street actions," like sits-in and marches, was coming to end. African Americans needed to be in positions of influence so they could design public policies and laws that addressed their needs.

In 1971, Barry was elected president of the District of Columbia school board. In 1974, he was elected to the city council. As chairman of the finance committee, he improved the city's finances and tax structure and reduced taxes for senior citizens by half.

In 1978, Barry became mayor of Washington, D.C. In that position, he opened up city government to those who had been excluded: senior citizens, the poor, gays, blacks, and others. Barry believed that the civil rights movement was not about skin color—it was about helping all Americans who were denied access to opportunities for a better life. During his twelve years as mayor, Barry revitalized the downtown area and brought many new jobs to the District of Columbia.

Unfortunately, Barry had problems with alcohol and drug addiction, which eventually cost him his position. He was sentenced to six months in jail. Some believed his political career was over, but Barry didn't agree. He worked his way back into public service by winning back people's trust. He worked closely with the people of Washington on issues that were important to them. In 1993, an article in the *Washington City Paper* said of Barry, "He walked the main streets, the side streets, the back streets and the back alleys of the ward."

Barry was reelected mayor of Washington, D.C., in 1994 in a landslide victory and served his full term, leaving office in 1999. Today, he continues to work hard for Americans as a lobbyist and consultant.

DR. JAMES LUTHER BEVEL

CIVIL RIGHTS LEADER
(1936–)

Nonviolence demands absolute truthfulness. . . . What makes absolute truthfulness so difficult is the embarrassment that comes upon us when we have to face and reveal the truth about our own personal errors, ill-will and ill-motivation.

James Bevel's grandfather was released from slavery in Selma, Alabama, in 1865. In the same city, one hundred years later, Bevel helped to organize a fight for freedom that was one of the most significant events in the civil rights movement.

Bevel was born on October 19, 1936, in Itta Bena, Mississippi. As soon as he was old enough, Bevel joined the military to serve his country. He could not ignore, however, the calling to join the ministry. When his tour of duty was over, he enrolled at the American Baptist Theological Seminary in Nashville, Tennessee. He also joined the Nashville Christian Leadership Conference (NCLC), the local arm of the Southern Christian Leadership Conference (SCLC).

The Reverend James Lawson trained NCLC members how to confront hate and violence with love and positive action. He taught them about the Indian leader Mohandas Gandhi and his philosophy of social change through nonviolent direct action. In Lawson's workshops, students practiced how to remain calm and respectful no matter how badly they were treated.

Because of this training, Lawson's students were well prepared for the abuse they suffered during their protests of the segregated restaurants in Nashville. Bevel was one of the student leaders during the sit-ins—along with Diane Nash (who later became Bevel's wife), James Lewis, Rev. C. T. Vivian, Marion Barry, and Bernard Lafayette.

Instead of protecting the protesters from violence, the police supported the segregationists. They watched as the angry mob beat up the students and dragged them from the lunch counters of Woolworth's and Kress department stores. Then they arrested the protesters and took them to jail. As soon as one group was hauled away, however, another group of NCLC volunteers took their seats, refusing to move.

The sit-ins continued from February to April. Hundreds of people were arrested, jailed, fined, released, and arrested—over and over again. Students and adults picketed, and the downtown stores lost thousands of dollars in business.

On April 19, 1960, an early morning bomb blast rocked the home of attorney Z. Alexander Looby, the city's most prominent civil rights attorney. Bevel, Nash, and others led a march of some four thousand residents to Mayor Ben West's office at city hall and demanded that he take action to stop the bombers. When confronted by the group, Mayor West admitted that discrimination was immoral and unacceptable—a shocking statement for a government official at that time.

Within weeks, the lunch counters and restaurants of downtown Nashville were open to all races. The successful sit-in campaign won the respect and support of both blacks and whites in Nashville. This great victory, and others like it, inspired African Americans across the nation to peacefully protest segregation in public places.

Bevel became chairman of the Nashville student movement and one of the founding members of the Student Nonviolent Coordinating Committee (SNCC). The SNCC changed the face of the civil rights movement by coordinating a series of peaceful, direct-action campaigns throughout the country.

Students were at the center of the civil rights movement. Unlike most adults, they did not have families to support or jobs they might lose as a result of their actions. Students stood up to turn the tide of racism. In 1961, the students' Freedom Rides, organized by the Congress of Racial Equality (CORE), met with resistance in Montgomery, Alabama. When the Freedom Riders were injured by violent mobs, Bevel, Lewis, Lafayette, and Barry traveled there with other members of the SNCC to continue the protest against segregated bus travel in the South.

In 1963, Bevel had the idea to enlist children in the SCLC's peaceful efforts to desegregate Birmingham, Alabama. All of America was shocked when Theophilus "Bull" Connor, Alabama's commissioner of public safety, unleashed fire hoses and police dogs on the young protesters. The televised images created enormous support for the movement and drew more volunteers—but unfortunately, the violence increased.

One of the most charged issues of the movement was voting rights, the most basic and fundamental of all rights in a democracy. Many Southern states had long-standing practices that made it difficult for blacks to register to vote. In 1962, Bevel created the SCLC Mississippi Project to help blacks exercise their voting rights in that state.

James Bevel standing on the Edmund Pettus Bridge

In 1963, about half of the voting-age population of Selma, Alabama, was African American. Of these 15,000 eligible voters, only 156 were registered. The SNCC, SCLC, and the NAACP took action in Selma to protect African Americans' right to vote.

During one demonstration, Bevel was arrested and beaten by sheriff's deputies for encouraging his five hundred fellow activists to sing protest songs. Some believe that the deputies may have attacked Bevel because they thought that his wife, Diane Nash, who was fair skinned, was a white woman. Bevel became ill with pneumonia after his abuse in the jail, which included the constant hosing down of his cell. After weeks of appeals from across the nation on his behalf, he was finally released for medical care.

In 1965, a peaceful march in Marion, Alabama, in support of voting rights suddenly turned violent. Jimmie Lee Jackson was shot and killed by state troopers while trying to protect his mother and eighty-two-year-old grandfather.

When Bevel heard about the incident, he proposed a protest march from Selma to the state capitol in Montgomery, a distance of more than fifty miles. The marchers intended to confront Alabama governor George Wallace, but Wallace stationed troops armed with riot gear to stop them. On Sunday, March 7—a day later known as Bloody Sunday—six hundred peaceful marchers were attacked by state troopers in gas masks on the Edmund Pettus Bridge. Troopers launched tear gas, and officers on horses beat the marchers with billy clubs.

Nationwide network programming was interrupted to show footage of police attacking the children, women, and men on the bridge. On March 15, President Lyndon B. Johnson announced a bill that would "strike down all restrictions used to deny the people the right to vote." The Voting Rights Act of 1965 became law.

Bevel went on to champion the Chicago housing movement in 1966. He protested against the Vietnam War in 1967 and joined in the Memphis sanitation workers' strike and the Poor People's Campaign of 1968. Today, Dr. James Bevel is pastor and adviser of the Hebraic-Christian-Islamic Assembly in Chicago, Illinois, where he continues to devote his energy to helping people recognize and live in truth.

DIANE NASH

CIVIL RIGHTS ACTIVIST, TENNESSEE
(1938–)

The movement had a way of reaching inside me and bringing out things that I never knew were there. Like courage, and love for people.

Diane Nash was born into a middle-class family in Chicago, Illinois, and attended college at Howard University in Washington, D.C. She had never experienced conditions like those in the segregated South until she transferred to Fisk University in Nashville, Tennessee.

Nash was outraged by the racist Jim Crow laws of the South. She was shocked to find segregated "colored only" restrooms, water fountains, and other public facilities. She talked to her fellow students about this unjust treatment, but they said they felt powerless to change the system.

One day, a classmate told Nash about James Lawson. Lawson, who had studied in India, was teaching activists in the growing civil rights movements. He was leading workshops in the nonviolent strategies of social change, based on the ideas of Indian leader Mohandas Gandhi. Nash studied with Lawson and became dedicated to the concept of peaceful resistance as a way to change society. In the workshops, Nash explained, "we would practice things such as how to protect your head from a beating, how to protect each other. . . . We would practice not striking back, if someone struck us."

In February 1960, students in Greensboro, North Carolina, organized peaceful sit-in protests at Woolworth's, a department store chain that refused to serve African Americans at their lunch counters. In support of these students, Nash organized another group of students to sit-in at the Woolworth's in Nashville. Students in other cities also organized sit-ins at Woolworth's.

Students across America began to realize they were not powerless. They saw that they could take a stand for civil rights without striking a blow. This realization marked the beginning of the nonviolent student actions at the center of the civil rights movement. In April 1960, Nash helped to found the Student Nonviolent Coordinating Committee (SNCC).

That spring, a bomb destroyed the home of Z. Alexander Looby, a civil rights attorney and Nashville's first African American city council member. Nash and students from campuses throughout the city marched to city hall to talk with Mayor Ben West. Nash directly confronted the mayor by asking, "Do you feel it is wrong to discriminate against a person solely on the basis of their race or color?" Surprisingly, the mayor admitted that he did. Soon after, the lunch counters of Nashville were desegregated. Nash continued to lead the direct-action wing of the SNCC with her friends John Lewis, Bernard Lafayette, and James Bevel.

In 1961, federal law prohibited segregation on interstate buses and in bus terminals. In many Southern states, however, segregated seating was required

FBI investigators at the 16th Street Baptist Church after the 1963 bombing

by law. James Farmer, the director of the Congress of Racial Equality (CORE), and twelve others decided to travel through Southern states by bus to enforce the federal law. They called their protests Freedom Rides. Angry whites staged violent protests against the Freedom Riders. Under Nash's leadership, SNCC members replaced those who were injured so the rides would continue. Nash believed that if the threat of violence stopped the Freedom Rides, the cause would be lost.

In 1962, the Southern Christian Leadership Conference (SCLC) hired Nash and her husband, James Bevel. The organization wanted them to bridge the communication gap between the young members of the SNCC and the older ministers of the SCLC. Nash, who was a master communicator, even reached out to the National Association for the Advancement of Colored People (NAACP), which feared the students' nonviolence campaign would damage the NAACP's legal strategy.

Nash said she laughed when people said they admired her courage and bravery. She said she always had "sweaty palms" before participating in sit-ins and marches. She was especially terrified of going to jail, which she did when she was four months pregnant. She had been sentenced to two years in prison for teaching children in Mississippi about nonviolent ways to respond to injustice. Nash appealed the sentence and was released.

In 1963, four young girls were killed in the bombing of the Sixteenth Street Church in Birmingham, Alabama. Nash immediately began to make plans. She was at the forefront of SNCC's Project C—the C stood for confrontation. She worked closely with Rev. Dr. Martin Luther King Jr. and Rev. Fred Shuttlesworth to plan a series of sit-ins and marches in Birmingham. She also organized nonviolent protests in Selma.

In 1963, President John F. Kennedy appointed Nash to a national committee to help review and strengthen the Civil Rights Act, which passed in 1964. In 1965, Martin Luther King presented Nash and Bevel with the SCLC's highest honor, the Rosa Parks Award.

After Stokely Carmichael took over the leadership of the SNCC in 1966, the organization moved away from the idea of nonviolent protest. Nash left the SNCC and returned to Chicago, where she worked for women's rights and fair housing.

In 2003, Nash received the Distinguished American Award from the John F. Kennedy Library and Foundation. In 2004, she received the LBJ Award for Leadership in Civil Rights from the Lyndon Baines Johnson Library and Museum. Today, she continues to work as an educator and lecturer committed to peace.

HORACE JULIAN BOND

CIVIL RIGHTS LEADER AND JOURNALIST
(1940–)

A voteless people voted with their bodies and their feet and paved the way for other social protests.

Horace Julian Bond was born January 14, 1940, in Nashville, Tennessee. In 1945, his father, Dr. Horace Mann Bond, was appointed the first black president of America's oldest private black college, Lincoln University in Pennsylvania. Bond attended the George School in Newtown, Pennsylvania, where he was first introduced to the Quaker faith. The Quakers, also known as the Religious Society of Friends, believe that all human beings are members of the same human family and that all members are equal.

In 1957, Bond entered Morehouse College in Atlanta, Georgia. He helped to start a literary magazine called the *Pegasus* and was employed as an intern for *Time* magazine. In 1960, the student sit-in movement swept through the black colleges of the South. Bond organized the Committee on Appeal for Human Rights (COHR), a student organization that directed student sit-ins and other antisegregation activities throughout Atlanta.

Later that same year, Ella Baker, the executive director of the Southern Christian Leadership Conference (SCLC) called a meeting at Shaw University in North Carolina. She gathered the student leaders of the sit-in campaigns across the country, including Bond, and formed the Student Nonviolent Coordinating Committee (SNCC). Soon after, Bond became the organization's communications director.

SNCC was one of the leading organizations of the civil rights movement. Its workers organized local demonstrations, marches, and voter registration drives. They traveled into the most racist regions of the South to explain the power and importance of voting to the African Americans living there.

The SNCC workers faced constant threat of violence from white segregationists. They were trained to escape lynch mobs and the white supremacist group, the Ku Klux Klan. Many SNCC field workers were murdered for trying to help black communities, but, year after year, more volunteers traveled to the South to help blacks register to vote and to organize against segregation.

As communications director, Bond created a publicity department, oversaw all the organization's printed materials, and edited its newsletter, the *Student Voice*. He also took part in protests and registration drives in the rural areas of Georgia, Alabama, Mississippi, and Arkansas.

In 1961, only one semester before graduation, Bond left Morehouse to join the staff of the *Atlanta Inquirer*, a new protest newspaper. Soon he became managing editor. Ten years later, Bond returned to Morehouse to finish his degree in English.

Meanwhile, to continue his work for civil rights, Bond decided to run for political office. In 1965, he was elected to the Georgia state legislature. The other members barred him from taking his seat, however, because he had spoken out against the war in Vietnam. In 1966, Bond was elected again, and again the Georgia House of Representatives voted to keep him out of the legislature. He won a third election, and this time, the U.S. Supreme Court ruled that the Georgia house had violated Bond's rights by refusing him his seat. Bond finally became a member of the lawmaking body of the state of Georgia in 1967.

Bond served for four terms (1967–1974) in the Georgia House of Representatives and for six terms (1974–1986) in the Georgia Senate. During that time, he sponsored or cosponsored sixty bills that became laws to improve living conditions for Georgians.

In 1968, Bond was the first African American to be nominated for the office of vice president of the United States by the national Democratic Party. According to the U.S. Constitution, however, a person has to be at least thirty-five years old to hold that office. Bond was not yet old enough, so he had to withdraw his name from the nomination.

Today, Bond continues to work for justice and civil rights. He served on the board of the National Association for the Advancement of Colored People (NAACP) from 1978 to 1979 and as chairman since 1998. "I've spent a lot of time learning about the history of the movement for civil rights in this country," he has said, "and it's clear that had there been no NAACP, this movement would not have progressed as far as quickly. . . . It was the NAACP that laid the ground upon which I stood when I sat in at lunch counters, when I picketed and marched and got arrested."

Bond is a Distinguished Scholar in Residence at American University in Washington, D.C., and a professor in the history department at the University of Virginia in Charlottesville. Bond is also the host of *America's*

Julian Bond (left) speaks out about being refused his seat in the Georgia House of Representatives.

Black Forum, the longest-running black-owned television show, which features discussion of social and political issues. The show has aired continuously since 1980 and is broadcast to more than two hundred stations nationwide. Bond's political and social commentaries are also published in "Viewpoint," his nationally syndicated newspaper column.

JOHN R. LEWIS
CIVIL RIGHTS LEADER, POLITICIAN
(1940–)

[The marches] represented America at her best. . . . There was the sense that we were one people, that we were one community, one family, the American family. . . . We had a mission to do what we could to make things better for all humankind.

John Lewis was born on February 21, 1940. He was the third of ten children in a family of sharecroppers near Troy, Alabama. Sometimes his father would ask the children to stay home from school to help plow a field or gather a crop. On those days, Lewis would get up early, get dressed, and hide under the front porch. When he heard the school bus coming, he'd take off running, catch the bus, and go to school. "I wanted to get an education because I knew I needed it, and I knew it would be better for me in the days and years to come," he later said.

During the days of the Montgomery Bus Boycott in 1955, Lewis listened to the speeches of Dr. Martin Luther King Jr. on the radio. The civil rights leader inspired the young boy. "I just felt that he was speaking to me," Lewis said. "Like he was saying, 'John Lewis, you can do it. You can get involved. You must get involved.' And when I got the chance, I got involved."

Lewis wanted to pattern his life after King's, so he decided to become a minister, too. He could not afford to go to Morehouse College, the school King attended. Instead, he went to American Baptist College in Nashville, Tennessee, and worked to pay his way through school.

Lewis was one of the first students to study with James Lawson. Lawson taught his students about the great religions of the world. He also taught them about the Indian leader Mohandas Gandhi and his successful nonviolent actions for social change. Most important, Lawson taught Lewis and his other students that one cannot create peace through violence.

In 1960, Lawson's students put their lessons to good use, as they conducted peaceful sit-ins and boycotts throughout Nashville. The success of student sit-ins led to the formation of the Student Nonviolent Coordinating Committee (SNCC), which was at the center of the civil rights movement.

In 1963, Lewis was elected national chairman of the SNCC. That year, he helped organize the historic March on Washington for Jobs and Freedom. He delivered a powerful speech to the crowd of more than 250,000 people.

In 1964, Lewis and the SNCC workers organized events during what came to be known as Freedom Summer. Mississippi was the stronghold of segregation in the South, and SNCC leaders believed that if they could "crack Mississippi," they stood a good chance of eliminating segregation throughout the nation. The SNCC brought thousands of college students of all races to Mississippi to register black voters.

During Freedom Summer, three SNCC workers were murdered, and many others were harassed and beaten. SNCC volunteers lived in constant fear for their lives. Some talked about responding with violence themselves or secretly carried guns. Lewis, however, never lost faith in the power of nonviolent action.

Selma, Alabama, was another segregationist stronghold. By 1965, SNCC workers had spent two years trying to register black voters. That spring, Dr. King arrived in Selma.

In advance, Dr. King had sent Hosea Williams as his representative, to work with John Lewis to plan a march from Selma to the state capitol in Montgomery. The purpose of the march was to focus media attention on Governor George Wallace. King hoped the attention would force the governor to stop the vicious attacks against blacks and allow African Americans to exercise their right to vote. Some SNCC resented the celebrity of King, who had become a national figure, and refused to take part—but Lewis joined him.

On Sunday, March 7, 1965, after church services, Lewis and Williams led the marchers out of Selma and across the Edmund Pettus Bridge over the Alabama River. Governor Wallace had sent armed troops to order the marchers to return to the church. Williams asked the officers if the marchers could first have a moment to pray together. As soon as the marchers knelt on the bridge, the troopers attacked. Lewis suffered a concussion and a fractured skull. "I became very concerned about the other people in the march, because I thought I was going to die. I just sort of said to myself, 'This is it. This is the end of the road for me. I'm going to die right here on this bridge,'" he remembered.

That night, video footage of the attack, which came to be known as Bloody Sunday, aired on news broadcasts across the country. Americans were outraged. The event finally convinced President Lyndon B. Johnson and Congress to pass the Voting Rights Act of 1965. The law protects the rights of all citizens to register and vote without fear of harassment or intimidation.

John Lewis is attacked by police on Bloody Sunday.

In 1966, under the new leadership of Stokely Carmichael, the SNCC became more militant in its actions. Lewis resigned, but he remained committed to his nonviolent efforts for civil rights. He once said, "You must not give up. You must not give in. You must not get lost in a sea of despair. Try to provide some sense of hope. I was beaten. I was arrested and jailed and all of that, but I don't hate anybody. I don't hold any malice and you must not."

In 1977, Lewis became director of the Voter Education Project, which helped some four million new black voters participate in the democratic process. In 1986, he was elected to Congress as a representative of Georgia, an office he still holds today. He has served on many important committees during his years in Congress and is a member of the Congressional Black Caucus.

JAMES ZWERG

CIVIL RIGHTS ACTIVIST

(1940–)

While we were attempting to integrate the movie theaters, there were situations where I'd get hit and kicked and spit on and this, that and the other thing. But I was also going through a transformation where nonviolence became more to me than just a technique. It became something that I deeply believed in, that changed my life.

James Zwerg had never even met an African American before he attended college. While at Beloit College in Wisconsin, Zwerg watched his black roommate, Robert Carter, face abuse again and again. Carter never lashed out verbally or physically. Zwerg, who had a short temper, didn't understand how Carter could deal so calmly with the unjust treatment. Carter said, "It doesn't prove anything," and gave Zwerg a copy of Dr. Martin Luther King Jr.'s book, *Stride toward Freedom.*

Zwerg became curious about the South. He applied to the exchange-student program so he could spend his junior year at Fisk University, an African American school in Nashville, Tennessee. There Zwerg met John Lewis, who was a member of the Student Nonviolent Coordinating Committee (SNCC) and organized student protests in support of civil rights. "I had never before encountered someone my age with such commitment," said Zwerg.

Through Lewis, Zwerg became involved with James Lawson's workshops. Lawson trained workshop participants in nonviolent methods of protest. His students role-played as protesters and antagonists to create hostile situations similar to what they might encounter during their demonstrations. Lawson trained the students how to withstand taunts and attacks. He also urged them never to respond to violence with violence. Zwerg learned that, "You can go to war, you can use some sort of weaponry, but the power of love is the only thing that can change people."

To test their training in nonviolent action, Zwerg and a black student, Bill Harbor, decided to try to integrate a "whites only" movie theater. Zwerg bought two tickets and handed one to Harbor. As Zwerg stepped inside the door, he was hit from behind with a monkey wrench and knocked out cold. His body was dragged out of the theater and left on the sidewalk.

Zwerg had more opportunities to test his training. He and others continued to try to integrate restaurants, theaters, parks, and other public places to which African Americans were denied equal access. Despite the violent resistance, the SNCC campaign finally succeeded in opening up Nashville's downtown restaurants and public areas to black citizens.

On May 4, 1961, a group of activists set out from Washington, D.C., on what they called Freedom Rides. Their goal was to enforce the laws against segregation on interstate buses. They were traveling to New Orleans, Louisiana, but angry mobs in Birmingham, Alabama, forced them to end

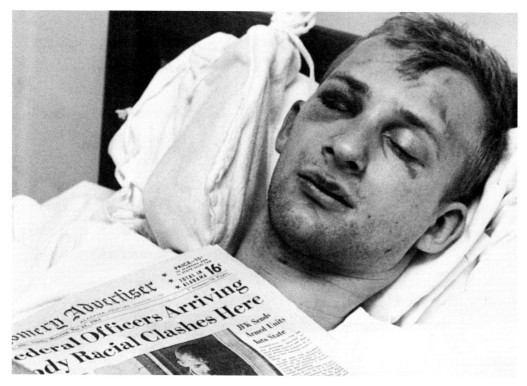

James Zwerg in a hospital after being attacked at the end of a Freedom Ride

their bus trip and fly the rest of the way. SNCC members in Nashville—including Zwerg—decided to go to Birmingham to continue the Freedom Rides. Several of them wrote notes to their families in case they did not survive the trip.

The SNCC members did not charter a bus like the previous group had. Instead, they bought tickets for the regular bus service and sat among the other passengers. They traveled to Birmingham without incident, but when they reached the Birmingham city limits, they were taken into "protective custody" by the police. The Alabama police drove them to the Tennessee state line and left them stranded there, without transportation, in the middle of the night.

As soon as they could, the students headed right back to Birmingham. Photographs of the mob violence had already aired on television and run in newspapers across the country. U.S. attorney general Robert F. Kennedy pressured the governor, state and local law enforcement officials, and the bus companies to protect the students as they continued their ride through Alabama to Montgomery. Kennedy promised that he would send in U.S. marshals to protect the students if the local officers did not.

With heavy police presence and planes flying overhead, the students rode safely to the Montgomery city limits. When the bus pulled into the Montgomery station, though, the police were not there. Instead, the students were met by an angry mob of several hundred people, armed with baseball bats, metal pipes, chains, and hammers.

Because he was white, Zwerg volunteered to step off the bus first to give the black riders a chance to escape. The crowd focused their anger on Zwerg, screaming, "Get the nigger-lover!" "I bowed my head," Zwerg said later, "and asked God to give me the strength and love that I would need, that I put my life in his hands, and to forgive them. And I had the most wonderful religious experience. I felt a presence as close to me as breath itself, if you will, that gave me peace knowing that whatever came, it was okay."

Zwerg was severely beaten long after he lost consciousness. Three of his vertebrae were cracked, his nose was broken, and, reportedly, men took turns trying to knock his teeth out. In an interview from his hospital bed, Zwerg said that, even though he could not join them, he felt the Freedom Riders should continue—and they did. More than three hundred Freedom Riders were arrested and jailed before the federal government finally enforced the laws against the segregation of interstate travel.

After spending five days in the hospital, Zwerg returned to Wisconsin. He finished school at Beloit College and went on to become a minister of the United Church of Christ.

STOKELY CARMICHAEL, A.K.A. KWAME TOURE

Civil Rights Leader
(1941–1998)

From birth, Black people are told a set of lies about themselves. We are told that we are lazy—yet I drive through the Delta area of Mississippi and watch Black people picking cotton in the hot sun for fourteen hours. We are told, 'If you work hard, you'll succeed'—but if that were true, Black people would own this country.

Stokely Carmichael was a most bold and passionate voice of the civil rights movement. With the two simple words "black power," he brought new energy into a community of people who were tired of waiting for change. Many whites and blacks believed his call for black power was a call for violence. Carmichael simply believed that, rather than sit and wait for America to change, African Americans should control their own communities, schools, and businesses.

Born on June 29, 1941, on the Caribbean island of Trinidad, Carmichael learned early about the fight for freedom. Trinidad was under British control, and by 1952, his father had grown tired of waiting for living conditions to improve. The family moved to the United States, settling first in Harlem and then in the East Bronx, New York.

Carmichael attended the prestigious Bronx High School of Science, but he was also curious about philosophy and different forms of government. In 1958 and 1959, he worked in Bayard Rustin's office to assist with the National Youth Marches for Integrated Schools. Rustin was a field director for the Congress of Racial Equality (CORE), an organization committed to nonviolent social change.

Carmichael began his freshman year at Howard University in Washington, D.C., in 1960—the year of the student sit-ins at segregated lunch counters throughout the South. He recalled, "One night when I saw those young kids on TV, getting back up on the lunch counter stools after being knocked off them, sugar in their eyes, ketchup in their hair—well, something happened to me. Suddenly I was burning." His political activism had begun.

Carmichael joined the Nonviolent Action Group (NAG), a political-action organization on the Howard University campus. In 1961, he volunteered to travel to Mississippi with the newly formed Student Nonviolent Coordinating Committee (SNCC). The SNCC members and volunteers were taking over the Freedom Rides for protesters who had been bombed, beaten, and arrested while riding buses through the segregated states of the South. Carmichael was also arrested. He was beaten repeatedly for forty-nine days in the penitentiary in Parchman, Mississippi.

Despite the brutal beatings that he suffered and the ongoing threat of violence, Carmichael returned to the South every summer to help people register to vote, to provide legal and medical assistance, and to help build Freedom Schools where black children could learn reading and math.

After Carmichael graduated from Howard University in 1964, he moved to Mississippi to work as a field organizer for the SNCC. Violence against African Americans had become a way of life in the South. To combat the fear and powerlessness that blacks felt, Carmichael helped organize the Lowndes County Freedom Organization. He made the fierce black panther its logo.

Carmichael always kept a stash of money hidden in the floor of his car so he would be prepared if fellow activists needed money for bail or fines. On June 16, 1966, he himself was arrested for the twenty-seventh time. After his release, Carmichael spoke to the crowd of three thousand gathered in a Greenwood, Mississippi, park: "I ain't going to jail no more. Every courthouse in Mississippi ought to be burned down. . . . We been saying 'Freedom' for six years, and we ain't got nothin'. What we gonna start saying now is Black Power!" The crowd chanted "black power" each time he asked them "What do you want?" "What do we need?"

Carmichael's speech marked a pivotal moment in the civil rights movement. African Americans had a new feeling of confidence and power. Carmichael's Black Power movement gained momentum as Dr. King's promise of peaceful change no longer seemed possible.

In 1967, Carmichael left the SNCC to join the Black Panther Party for Self-Defense, founded in California by Huey Newton and Bobby Seale. In 1968, he was named the "prime minister" of the party. The Black Panthers wanted to build alliances with whites, but Carmichael disagreed. He had come to believe that blacks could only thrive in their own separate society. In 1969, he left the Black Panther Party. He and his wife, African-born singer and activist Miriam Makeba, moved to Guinea, Africa.

Stokely Carmichael (center, pointing to ground) at a 1967 protest in Alabama

Carmichael had made his first trip to Guinea in 1967. There he met Ghana's former president Kwame Nkrumah, who had been overthrown by a military uprising. Carmichael began to see a connection between the black struggles for freedom in the United States and those in Africa. Nkrumah later appointed Carmichael head of his All African Peoples Revolutionary Party. In 1969, Carmichael accepted a position as political secretary to Guinea's prime minister, Ahmed Sekou Toure.

In 1978, Carmichael changed his name to Kwame Toure. He chose the name *Kwame* to honor his mentor, Kwame Nkrumah, who led Ghana into independence in 1957. He chose the name *Toure* to honor Guinea's head of state. A true civil rights hero, Kwame Toure continued to travel to the United States to promote his message of African unity and spent the rest of his life fighting for the liberation of African peoples.

JESSE LOUIS JACKSON SR.

CIVIL RIGHTS LEADER, POLITICIAN

(1941–)

A man must be willing to die for justice. Death is an inescapable reality and men die daily, but good deeds live forever.

Born on October 8, 1941, in Greenville, South Carolina, Jesse Jackson was raised by his mother, Helen, and his stepfather, Charles Jackson, who adopted Jesse. As a young man, Jackson was an athlete and also an A student. He won a scholarship to attend the University of Illinois, but did not feel welcome on the predominantly white campus. When the football team's coach refused to let him play the position of quarterback, Jackson transferred to a historically African American school, North Carolina Agricultural and Technical State University in Greensboro.

During his time there, Jackson developed his natural skills as a leader. His good looks, confidence, and negotiation skills made him popular on campus. He played quarterback for the team and was a National Honor Society student. He was also president of his fraternity and the student body.

Jackson had begun school in the fall of 1960, just after the famous Greensboro sit-ins that integrated the lunch counters in the segregated South. These events marked the start of the student movement—and the start of Jackson's life as a civil rights activist. That year, he joined the local chapter of the Congress of Racial Equality (CORE).

In the South at that time, blacks were not allowed into movie theaters, restaurants, and other public places frequented by whites. In 1963, Jackson organized sit-ins, marches, and mass arrests to protest segregation. He led demonstrations at downtown locations, such as the Old Mayfair and S&W Cafeteria. That year, he also met Jacqueline Davis, who joined the student protests and later became Jackson's wife.

In 1964, Jackson graduated from college and received a Rockefeller Grant to attend the Chicago Theological Seminary. In 1965, he traveled to Selma, Alabama, to protest for equal voting rights alongside civil rights leaders Rev. Dr. Martin Luther King Jr. and Rev. Ralph Abernathy. When the two leaders began to make plans for the Chicago Freedom Movement in 1966, they asked Jackson to help.

Jackson left the seminary and joined the Southern Christian Leadership Conference (SCLC), the civil rights organization founded by King, Abernathy, and other church leaders. He organized the local ministers and led a march through all-white communities of Chicago, demanding equal housing opportunities for African Americans.

King then asked Jackson to coordinate Operation Breadbasket. Jackson urged Chicago's black community to support African American–owned businesses and to boycott white businesses that refused to hire black workers or sell ethnic products. A year later, Jackson became national director of

Operation Breadbasket. Under his leadership, the project created many changes in Chicago. A large exposition was established to promote African American businesses and manufacturers. Dairies and supermarkets hired more African Americans, and big business and government agencies made deposits in African American banks.

Jackson did not receive his degree in divinity until 2000, but he was ordained as a minister in 1968, the year that King was assassinated. Jackson was with King at the Lorraine Motel, in Memphis, Tennessee, that day. The two men were telling jokes and talking only moments before King was killed by an assassin's bullet.

After King's death, Abernathy took over leadership of the SCLC. Jackson and Abernathy had differences of opinion about SCLC policy and programs, so Jackson resigned from the SCLC in 1971. That year, he founded his own organization, called People United to Save Humanity (PUSH).

Jackson wanted to take direct action to protect African American homeowners and support African American families and businesses. He organized marches against hunger, which resulted in more government funding for school lunches. He also created a PUSH-Excel Program to help teens finish school and find jobs.

In 1986, Jackson founded the Rainbow Coalition. The organization invited people of all races, beliefs, and backgrounds to work together to pursue "liberty and justice for all." In 1996, he merged his two organizations, now known as RainbowPUSH, to create a stronger organization.

Jackson has campaigned twice for the Democratic presidential nomination—in 1984 and 1988. In his 1988 campaign, he exposed several issues, such as homelessness, the drug crisis in America, and the need for a higher minimum wage and for a better day care system for children of working mothers. The nomination that year went to his opponent, Michael Dukakis, but Jackson received more than 6.9 million votes.

The District of Columbia has been seeking to become its own state since 1984. To further the cause, it created the position of statehood senator. Jackson was elected as statehood senator in 1990 and served a six-year term.

For the past three decades, Jackson has fought and won battles with big business, challenging unfair employment practices and discrimination in the workplace. With his Wall Street Project, he encourages youth to take part in corporate America so they can influence hiring practices and company policies. "We don't want to be just consumers and workers," Jackson has said, "but investors and partners."

Jackson has traveled throughout the world on peacekeeping missions. In 1990, he was the first American to bring hostages out of Iraq and Kuwait. He has negotiated the release of political prisoners in Cuba and of an African American navy pilot held hostage in Syria. Jackson also visited Yugoslav president Slobodan Milosevic and successfully arranged the release of three captured U.S. soldiers in 1999. His historic rescues have earned him worldwide respect and admiration as an advocate for human rights.

As Rev. Jackson continues his work, his simple but memorable poem "I Am Somebody" delivers a message of hope to all people who are struggling and oppressed: "Hold your head high, stick your chest out. You can make it. It gets dark sometimes, but morning comes. Keep hope alive."

EMMETT TILL

INNOCENT VICTIM
(1941–1955)

Have you ever sent a live son on vacation and had him returned to you in a pine box, so horribly battered and water-logged that someone needs to tell you this sickening sight is your son—lynched?
—Mamie Bradley

The 1954 *Brown v. Board of Education* decision provided the legal basis for the civil rights movement. The murder of fourteen-year-old Emmett Till provided the moral one.

Emmett Till was born on July 25, 1941, in Chicago, Illinois, to Mamie Bradley and Louis Till. In the summer of 1955, Emmett left the city of Chicago to visit relatives in Money, Mississippi, a town with a population of only fifty-five. Till's mother explained that he needed to behave differently in the South than he did in the North. He had to always say, "Yes sir" and "No sir." He must never look at a white woman and must step off the sidewalk to let her pass.

Till and his cousin Curtis Jones were spending the summer in Money with their adult cousin, a sharecropper named Moses "Preacher" Wright. Jones, who was also from Chicago, described Till as a practical joker. One day, the two boys went to Bryant's Grocery and Meat Market, where they talked and played checkers outside with some of the local boys they had met. Till showed the boys a picture of a white girl and claimed she was his girlfriend. One of the boys dared him to speak to the white female shopkeeper in the store. Till went inside to buy candy and, as he left, he reportedly said to her, "Bye Baby."

The shopkeeper's husband, Roy Bryant, was out of town that day. When he later heard about the young boy's comment to his wife, he decided that Till had crossed the color line. Three days later, Bryant and his brother-in-law J. W. Milam went to Moses Wright's house to find the youth. Wright begged the men not to take the boy, explaining it was only Till's second summer in the South and that he didn't know any better. Bryant and Milam threatened Wright. Then they kidnapped, tortured, and beat his young cousin.

The two men drove Till to the Tallahatchie River, where they made him remove his clothes. They forced him to carry a 75-pound (34-kilogram) cotton-gin fan to the river's edge and then they shot him in the head. Till's body was found in the river three days later, with the fan tied to his neck by barbed wire. When Wright was asked to identify the brutalized corpse, he could only identify his cousin by the engraved ring on the boy's finger, which once belonged to Till's father.

Bryant and Milam were arrested for murder. The young boy was so badly disfigured the sheriff wanted to bury his body immediately, but Till's mother insisted that her son's body be returned to Chicago. The sheriff sent Till's remains with an order that the casket not be opened. Mamie Bradley defied the order, however, and opened the pine box. She was horrified at the sight of her mutilated child. She wanted the world to see what happened to her son in Mississippi. So she had his body displayed for public viewing for four days. More than one hundred thousand members of the black community stood in line for hours to witness what had happened to Emmett Till.

The headline on the front page of the *Chicago Defender* read, "Nation Shocked, Vow Action in Lynching of Chicago Youth." Scores of journalists from the North invaded the small town of Money. A photograph of Till's tortured remains was published in *Jet* magazine and in African American and white newspapers throughout the country. The photograph caused an outpouring of sympathy and anger. White Northerners criticized the South for its Jim Crow laws and violent practices, and African Americans demanded change.

In those days, the murder of an African American, especially in the South, was not considered an important matter. African Americans who openly accused a white man of killing a black man were risking their own lives. For that reason, Curtis Jones's mother would not allow her son to return to Mississippi to testify at the trial. Although Moses Wright received warnings and death threats to his family, he did testify against Bryant and Milam. His courage brought forth other witnesses.

An all-white, male jury declared Bryant and Milam "not guilty," although the two men admitted to the kidnapping and murder later. Many people were angered by the decision, but few were surprised. In 1955, a white man had never been convicted of killing an African American. The verdict launched demonstrations in several major cities, and Northern blacks called for a march of protest on Mississippi.

The media compared the conditions for African Americans in the Mississippi Delta to those for the Jewish people in Europe during World War II. At that time, Jewish people and other ethnic groups were regularly threatened, imprisoned, tortured, and killed. Some called Emmett Till the

Emmett Till's mother weeps as his body is lowered into its grave.

"Anne Frank of America." Anne Frank was a German-Jewish teenager who died in a prison camp in Germany at age fifteen. She wrote about her experiences in her diary, which was later published as a book called *The Diary of a Young Girl*.

After the trial, Wright and his family moved to Chicago. In fact, large numbers of African Americans and white Americans began to leave Mississippi. The Bryants returned to their grocery business, but without the patronage of African American customers, they were forced to close the store and move to Texas.

Mamie Bradley began telling her tragic story to audiences across America and urged people to get involved. "When something happened to Negroes in the South I said, 'That's their business, not mine.' Now I know how wrong I was. The murder of my son has shown me that what happens to any of us, anywhere in the world, had better be the business of us all." With the murder of Emmett Till, the modern civil rights movement had begun.

DR. JAMES EDWARD ORANGE

CIVIL RIGHTS ACTIVIST, ALABAMA

(1942–)

*We all have to get together as brothers and sisters,
or we will perish together.*

The Reverend Dr. James Edward Orange joined the frontlines of the civil rights movement the night he had attended a mass meeting for the Alabama Improvement Association. His original motive for being there was to meet a young woman who sang in the choir. The two had planned to go out for sodas following the service.

The church pews were filled, except for two benches in the front. Orange sat down and listened to a sermon by Rev. Ralph Abernathy. "The longer I listened," Orange said, "the more intently I listened as I became absorbed in his message. It was nineteen sixty-two and the movement was determined to break segregation in Birmingham, the city of Sheriff 'Bull' Connor and his police dogs."

When the sermon was finished, the audience gave Abernathy a standing ovation. A man from the association asked those who were willing to join their effort to step forward. "I was already up front," Orange said, "and, a few minutes later, found myself, together with those who had come forward, in the church basement. Although I didn't know it yet, the trip down those stairs changed my life forever." Orange had joined the fight against segregation and the Jim Crow laws of the South. "There was no turning back," he said.

Orange was a large man, weighing 300 pounds (136 kg) and standing more than 6 feet (1.8 m) tall. His first task was to lead eight protesters who were going to picket a local market. Unaware that the group legally had to remain on the sidewalk while picketing, Orange led the group inside the store. The police soon arrived and arrested all of them.

Orange would be arrested more than a hundred times while working for the civil rights movement. He became one of the first full-time organizers of the Southern Christian Leadership Conference (SCLC), a group of church leaders committed to nonviolent protest for social change.

Orange was a dynamic leader. In 1968, after the assassination of civil rights leader Dr. Martin Luther King Jr., he played a key role in the Poor People's Campaign that King had hoped to lead. The purpose of the campaign was to pressure Congress and other governmental agencies to create an "economic bill of rights." Orange arranged for more than three hundred busloads of participants to arrive at the Washington, D.C., event. The gathering of some twenty-five hundred people brought the struggle of the poor in America to the attention of the nation. Some believe the campaign led to the establishment of the Food Stamp Program, which helps those in need buy food.

In 1977, Orange left the SCLC to work with labor unions. He joined the organizing campaign of the Amalgamated Clothing and Textile Workers Union and was later assigned to the American Federation of Labor and Congress of Industrial Organizations (AFL-CIO). Orange coordinated labor campaigns throughout the South, which helped pass the Workplace Fairness Bill. He also argued several cases before the National Labor Relations Board, leading to positive changes for workers.

Throughout his career, Orange maintained his commitment to the theories of nonviolence he learned while with the SCLC. In 1992, he worked with gangs in Atlanta, Georgia, to negotiate a truce. When the city of Atlanta hosted the 1994 Olympics, Orange trained a team in nonviolent techniques for monitoring public safety and controlling crowds during the Games.

In 1994, when South Africa had its first free elections, Orange made several trips there to assist in the election of Nelson Mandela as the country's first black president. In 2002, he was appointed to serve as the ambassador to the Republic of South Africa by the Georgia Association of Black Elected Officials. Today, Orange serves as the community and religious coordinator for the AFL–CIO Southern Region in Atlanta.

DR. BERNICE JOHNSON REAGON

CIVIL RIGHTS ACTIVIST, SINGER, COMPOSER, AND SCHOLAR
(1942–)

I learned that if you bring black people together, you bring them together with a song. To this day, I don't understand how people think they can bring anybody together without a song.

During the sit-ins, marches, bus rides, and rallies of the civil rights movement, African Americans found courage in the words of old Negro spirituals. Bernice Johnson Reagon once said, "The voice I have now, I got the first time I sang in a movement meeting, after I got out of jail. . . . and I'd never heard it before in my life."

Bernice, who was born in Albany, Georgia, on October 4, 1942, grew up singing in her father's church. "My first instruments were my hands and feet," she once said. In 1961, she was a student at Albany State College. She was

Bernice Johnson Reagon (seated, center) with Sweet Honey In The Rock in 1990

also a member of the Albany chapter of the Youth Council of the National Association for the Advancement of Colored People (NAACP).

As in other parts of the country, the civil rights movement in Albany gained momentum because of college students. In November 1961, several local African American organizations came together to form the Albany Movement. They elected William G. Anderson, a young osteopath (doctor of natural medicine) as their president, and gave the call for action. A demonstration in December led to the arrests of more than five hundred protesters, including Bernice. During her overnight stay in jail, she sang songs to comfort herself.

In 1962, not long after her release from prison, Bernice and three other activists founded the Freedom Singers. The quartet also included Charles Neblitt, Rutha Harris, and Cordell Hull Reagon. They performed spirituals, hymns, and gospel music. As members of the Student Nonviolent Coordinating Committee (SNCC), their goal was to incite social activism through music. The Freedom Singers raised money for the SNCC and helped give African Americans the inspiration and courage to keep fighting.

The Freedom Singers had no need for an organ or piano. They sang a cappella style, relying only on their own voices. With no musical instruments to carry, it was easy for them to travel. Between 1962 and 1963, they traveled 100,000 miles (160,934 km) in an old Buick station wagon to perform at rallies and marches and in churches and universities. The songs they performed became themes for the civil rights movement—"This Little Light of Mine," "Ain't Scared of Nobody," "Oh Freedom," "We Shall Overcome," and many others.

Reagon was suspended from Albany State College for her participation in the civil rights movement. She married fellow singer and activist Cordell Hull Reagon, and after she had her two children, she decided it was time to come off the road. "Life's challenges are not supposed to paralyze you," she said, "they're supposed to help you discover who you are."

Sweet Honey In The Rock performing in 2004

In 1970, Reagon earned her bachelor's degree in history from Spelman College in Atlanta, Georgia. Three years later, she founded Sweet Honey In The Rock, an a cappella ensemble. The all-female vocal group today travels throughout the world, singing songs that protest injustice. Until she retired from the group in 2004, Reagon produced and composed much of the music for the sextet. She wrote "Ella's Song" as a tribute to civil rights leader Ella Baker: "We who believe in freedom cannot rest, We who believe in freedom cannot rest until it comes." The group has made many recordings and won a Grammy Award for its contributions to music.

In 1974, Reagon earned a doctorate in U.S. history from Howard University. A specialist in protest traditions, performance, and the oral history of African Americans, she has published several articles and books on those topics.

From 1974 to 1993, she served as folklorist, program director, and curator for the Smithsonian Institution in Washington, D.C. In 1993, she was named curator emerita of the Smithsonian Institution's National Museum of American History. From 1993 to 2002, she was a professor of history at American University.

In 1992, Reagon produced and narrated the Peabody Award–winning radio series *Wade in the Water, African American Sacred Music Traditions* and the Emmy-nominated PBS documentary *The Songs Are Free: Bernice Johnson Reagon with Bill Moyers*. In 1989, she received a MacArthur Foundation Fellowship, also known as a "genius grant."

In 1995, President Bill Clinton presented Dr. Reagon with the Charles Frankel Prize, one of the nation's top honors, for her contribution to the public understanding of the humanities. She once said, "I don't accept the world the way it works. I take on the world. I want to make the world the way it should be."

THE WOMEN OF THE MONTGOMERY BUS BOYCOTT

Jo Ann Robinson, Claudette Colvin, and Rosa Parks
(1955)

More and more of our people are already arranging with neighbors and friends to ride to keep from being insulted and humiliated by bus drivers. . . . We, sir, do not feel that forceful measures are necessary in bargaining for a convenience which is right for all bus passengers.
—*Jo Ann Robinson, in a letter to Mayor W. A. Gayle of Montgomery, Alabama, May 21, 1954*

The Montgomery Bus Boycott was one of the most significant events of the civil rights movement. It was also the longest-running protest of Americans against injustice in the twentieth century. At the center of this powerful, nonviolent protest were three exceptional women: Jo Ann Robinson, Claudette Colvin, and Rosa Parks.

During the Jim Crow days of the South, Southern cities had specific laws that forbid blacks and whites from sitting together on buses. The laws reserved the front seats of the bus for whites only. Blacks could only sit in the back of the bus. If the bus was full and a white person wanted to sit down, an African American passenger would have to give up a seat.

In 1949, a white bus driver yelled at Jo Ann Robinson, a professor of English at the University of Alabama, for accidentally sitting in the all-white section of the bus. Robinson tried to organize a boycott of bus travel to protest the humiliation and abuse of African Americans on the buses of Montgomery. She could not gather enough support from other black citizens, however, so she had to postpone her plan. In the meantime, she continued her work with the Women's Political Council (WPC), an organization of professional woman working for civil rights, which she had cofounded. Finally, Robinson had the opportunity to put her plan into action.

On March 2, 1955, a fifteen-year-old high school student named Claudette Colvin was dragged from a bus by two police officers for refusing to give up her seat to a white passenger. The girl was handcuffed and taken to jail.

Leaders of the National Association for the Advancement of Colored People (NAACP) wanted to take Colvin's case to court. They saw her arrest as an opportunity to prove to a judge that segregation was illegal. When they learned that Colvin was pregnant and unmarried, however, they abandoned the idea. They felt the press would portray Colvin in a negative light and hurt the case—but, as Colvin said later, her decision to remain seated "was a spark, and it caught on."

On December 1 of that same year, Rosa Parks, a forty-three-year-old seamstress, was also asked to give up her seat to a white man who was left standing. She, too, refused. "Well if you don't stand up, I'm going to have to call the police and have you arrested," the bus driver said. Parks calmly responded, "You may do that."

The bus on which Rosa Parks refused to give up her seat

That same night, civil rights attorney Fred Gray contacted Jo Ann Robinson to notify her of Parks's arrest. The court date was set for Monday, December 5. Robinson had only three days to write and mimeograph thirty-five thousand flyers announcing a one-day bus boycott on the day of the court date. She secretly distributed them in schools, stores, bars, and churches.

Edgar Daniel Nixon, who headed the local chapter of the NAACP, raised money to get Parks out of prison on bond. Parks had worked with Nixon when she was secretary of the Montgomery branch of the NAACP. Nixon asked her if she would be willing to let the NAACP feature her case in its efforts to break down the segregation laws. Parks agreed.

Robinson delivered flyers to a meeting of the International Ministerial Association to tell them about the one-day boycott. She asked them to consider a longer boycott, and the group met that night to make a decision.

The Reverend L. Roy Bennett asked for the ministers' full support of the boycott, but many of them wanted to debate the issue. Half of the ministers left the meeting, but the rest agreed to support Monday's boycott.

Nixon took one of Robinson's flyers to a white reporter to get press coverage, and a story appeared in that Sunday's edition of the *Montgomery Advertiser.* Monday morning, the South Jackson bus, which was usually full of African Americans, was empty—and so was the next bus, and the next.

The afternoon of December 5, Rosa Parks was found guilty of breaking the segregation law and received a suspended sentence. She was fined ten dollars and four dollars in court fees.

Some ministers and community leaders believed that the boycott should end after its one-day success. Nixon challenged them to stand up for the citizens who traveled by bus every day. "The time has come when you men is going to have to learn to be grown men or scared boys," he said.

Boycott organizers wanted to show the city that black citizens were serious about improving conditions in Montgomery. They formed an organization called the Montgomery Improvement Association (MIA). Rev. Rufus Lewis nominated twenty-six-year-old Martin Luther King Jr. as the association's first president. The MIA decided to let the citizens themselves decide whether or not the boycott should continue.

The evening of December 5, five thousand people filled the Holt Street Baptist Church, and thousands more stood outside listening to the discussion through loudspeakers. After a stirring speech by Dr. King, the crowd voted unanimously to continue the boycott.

At that meeting, the MIA outlined the demands they would present to the city. Among them was that bus drivers treat black passengers courteously. They also asked for black bus drivers and for a seating system based on a first-come, first-served policy—even though African Americans would still fill the bus from back to front.

On December 8, after three more days of the boycott, the MIA presented the resolution to National City Lines, the company that owned the Montgomery bus lines. James Bagley, the bus company manager, and Jack Crenshaw, the company's attorney, refused the MIA's requests. So the boycott continued.

Whites who supported the cause also stopped riding the bus. So many buses were empty that eventually the company had to fire many of its drivers. The city threatened to fine black taxi drivers if they let passengers ride for a lower fare or for free. The MIA enlisted volunteers to transport the boycotters to and from their jobs.

The boycott continued for weeks, and white resistance grew. The police began giving tickets for minor infractions to volunteers who provided transportation to the boycotters. People waiting for rides were arrested for hitchhiking. Segregationists fired gunshots at buses. On January 30, Dr. King's home was bombed. The next day, Nixon's was, too.

The MIA decided to seek justice from the courts. On February 1, Fred Gray filed suit on behalf of five women, including Claudette Colvin and Rosa Parks, who had been arrested for refusing to give up seats on the bus. In June, the U.S. District Court ruled in favor of the women.

White segregationists tried again to force an end to the boycott. They pressured insurance agents throughout the South to cancel policies on cars that were transporting boycotters. The mayor even got a restraining order to keep boycotters from gathering on street corners to wait for their rides, claiming that their singing was a public nuisance.

On December 20, 1956, the official order from the U.S. Supreme Court arrived in Montgomery, declaring that segregation on the city's buses was unconstitutional. The thirteen-month-long boycott finally ended. Inspired by the success in Montgomery, African Americans in Birmingham and Mobile, Alabama, and in Tallahassee, Florida, found the courage to begin their own boycotts.

THE GREENSBORO FOUR

FRANKLIN McCain, Joseph McNeil, Ezell Blair Jr., and David Richmond

(1960)

I was fully prepared mentally not to ever come back to the campus. . . .
I thought the worst thing that could happen to us is we could have
had our heads split open with a nightstick and hauled into prison.
—Franklin McCain

The Greensboro Four (from left: Richmond, McCain, Blair, and McNeil)

In 1960, four students in North Carolina—Franklin McCain, Joseph McNeil, Ezell Blair Jr., and David Richmond—decided to take action. They were freshmen on academic scholarships at North Carolina Agricultural and Technical University in Greensboro. They decided to stop talking about the terrible conditions for blacks in the South and do something about it. The four men had read a handout distributed by the Congress of

Racial Equality (CORE) that outlined techniques for nonviolent protest. They decided to stage a sit-in.

At that time, Woolworth's was a national chain of department stores. At Woolworth's stores in the North, blacks and whites sat and ate together at the lunch counters, but at stores in the South, blacks had to eat outside or at a separate, stand-up snack bar. On February 1, McCain, McNeil, Blair, and Richmond—later known as the Greensboro Four—decided to change that.

First, the men each purchased a small item at the store. Then they took seats next to each other at the lunch counter and waited. A dozen or so white customers also sat down. At first, everyone just ignored the black men. Finally, the waitress told the students that Woolworth's did not serve black people at the counter, and she asked them to leave. The four men refused to move.

An African American store employee came over to the men and lectured them on their behavior, explaining it would hurt race relations in Greensboro. Still, the four refused to go. The store manager, Curly Harris, walked to the police station and reported the incident to the police chief, Paul Calhoun. The chief said that as long as the four men behaved, there wasn't anything he could do, but he sent an officer to the store to watch the situation.

An elderly white woman at the counter approached the students and patted McCain on the shoulder. "Boys," she said, "I am just so proud of you. My only regret is that you didn't do this ten or fifteen years ago." McCain later said, "That simple acknowledgment and pat on the shoulder meant more to me that day than anything else. . . . I got so much pride and such a good positive feeling from that little old lady. I mean, she'll never know it, but that really made the day for us."

The store manager, frustrated that the men still wouldn't leave, finally just closed the lunch counter. The students left peacefully, but told him they would be back the next day. Back on campus, the four men told other

Four African American students (from left: McNeil, McCain, Billy Smith, Clarence Henderson) the second day of the Woolworth's protest

students what they had done. At first, no one believed them. Finally, a few volunteers agreed to participate in the sit-in the next day.

The Greensboro Four went back to Woolworth's on February 2. Only two other students showed up to support them. The six men sat at the lunch counter for four hours without being served. Angry white hecklers hurled insults at them, but the students left without being arrested or harmed. The local news station sent a cameraman and the local newspapers sent reporters to cover the event.

When news of the demonstration hit the media, students from the surrounding colleges flocked to join the sit-in at Woolworth's and begin another at the lunch counter at the nearby Kress five-and-ten store.

On day four, black and white students occupied all the seats at the lunch counter. Others set up picket lines outside the store and paraded along the sidewalks. There were protests at all the segregated restaurants in

Greensboro. By day seven, there were sit-ins in fifteen cities in nine states throughout the South.

The sit-ins continued in Greensboro, off and on, for five months before the two chains—Woolworth's and Kress—finally agreed to desegregate the lunch counters in all their stores. These two companies had stores in virtually every major city in the nation. The first African Americans to eat at the newly integrated Woolworth's lunch counter in Greensboro were three of the store's black employees, although there were no reporters or photographers to record the event.

More than seventy thousand people took part in the lunch counter sit-ins. Students held similar events as far north as Ohio and west to Nevada to protest segregation of swimming pools, bus and train stations, parks, museums, art galleries, beaches, and other public places.

To help organize the efforts of the students, Ella Baker, executive director of the Southern Christian Leadership Council (SCLC) called a meeting of the leaders of the various sit-ins. They gathered at Shaw University in Raleigh, North Carolina. From this meeting came a new organization, called the Student Nonviolent Coordinating Committee (SNCC). Baker empowered the students to set their own agenda, rather than follow the direction of the SCLC or another established organization. The SNCC grew to be a powerful, independent force in the movement for American civil rights.

The Greensboro Four ushered in a new era in the civil rights struggle. No longer satisfied to simply wait for change, students across the country took peaceful, direct action. By doing so, they drew national attention and inspired tens of thousands of Americans of all races to take an active role in the movement for civil rights.

THE FREEDOM RIDES

(1961)

We were told that the racists, the segregationists, would go to any extent to hold the line on segregation in interstate travel. . . . So when we began the ride I think all of us were prepared for as much violence as could be thrown at us. We were prepared for the possibility of death.
—*James Farmer*

The Freedom Rides were acts of protest against segregation on interstate travel. In the South during the 1940s, it was common practice to have separate seating for blacks and whites on buses and trains. In 1944, Irene Morgan began a Greyhound bus trip in the North, which did not have segregated seating. When her bus passed through Virginia, she was arrested for not obeying the state's segregation laws.

In 1946, the U.S. Supreme Court heard her case. The Court decided that it was unreasonable to stop buses and trains that traveled from the North to the

South in order to force passengers to change their seats. In *Morgan v. The Commonwealth of Virginia,* the Court ruled that segregated interstate travel violated the U.S. Constitution.

Travel remained segregated in the South, however. Bus ride protests began in 1947 to force those states to uphold the Supreme Court decision. Bayard Rustin and James Farmer, leaders of the Congress of Racial Equality (CORE), organized what they called the Journey of Reconciliation. Nine CORE volunteers—three black and six white—rode buses through the upper South. The whites rode in the seating reserved for blacks, and the blacks rode in the "whites only" section.

In some places along the way, the volunteers were attacked and beaten. In others, they were arrested, fined, and jailed. In North Carolina, several of them, including Rustin, were sentenced to thirty days of hard labor on a chain gang for daring to disobey the state's segregation laws.

In 1961, CORE was ready to try again. President John F. Kennedy, who had won the presidential election with the support of black voters, showed little interest in the effort to desegregate travel—but Farmer and CORE leaders knew they had the law on their side.

On May 4, a group of thirteen people, black and white, left Washington, D.C., and headed by bus to New Orleans, Louisiana. They planned to arrive on May 17, the seventh anniversary of the U.S. Supreme Court's *Brown v. Board of Education* decision, which led to the integration of public schools. Some of the volunteers wrote letters to their families in case they were killed on the trip. The volunteers were known as Freedom Riders.

There were only a few small incidents in Virginia and the Carolinas, when riders tried to use the bus terminal restrooms and lunch counters. In Atlanta, Georgia, the Freedom Riders decided to split into two groups before they traveled through Alabama. One group headed for Anniston, and the other to Birmingham.

When the first group arrived at the Anniston bus depot, their bus was attacked. A mob of some two hundred racists threw stones and slashed the tires. The quick-thinking driver pulled out of the station and sped away on flat tires. When he stopped the bus 6 miles (9.7 km) outside of town to change the tires, another mob surrounded the bus and attacked again. Someone threw a firebomb. The Freedom Riders rushed out the emergency exit, and within moments, the bus was aflame. The next day, newspapers all across America ran a photograph of that fiery bus on their front pages.

The second bus met a similar fate. An informant had warned the Federal Bureau of Investigation (FBI) that there was a plan for another attack in Birmingham. Still, the FBI did not send anyone to protect the riders, and the local police purposely stayed away.

Despite the violence, the Freedom Riders were not willing to give up. The bus company, however, was not willing to lose any more buses, and the bus drivers were not willing to risk their lives. The Freedom Riders were unable to continue. Fearing more mob violence, they got on a plane and flew to New Orleans.

When they heard what had happened, students in Nashville, Tennessee, headed to Birmingham to continue the Freedom Rides. U.S. attorney general Robert Kennedy persuaded the Greyhound bus line to carry the riders. He also pressured Alabama governor John Patterson to take steps to protect them. Patterson agreed to provide an escort of state highway patrol to guard the bus and a plane to fly above it for the entire trip.

On May 20, the Freedom Riders and their police escort left Birmingham and headed for Montgomery. As they approach the city limits, the police pulled away. The ride was quiet until the bus pulled into the Montgomery bus terminal, where a mob was waiting. One of the riders, James Zwerg, who was white, stepped off the bus first and was dragged into the mob and severely beaten. Attorney General Kennedy's aide John Seigenthaler, who had escorted

Freedom Riders being taken into police custody in Jackson, Mississippi

the bus in a rental car, tried to save several women by hurrying them into his vehicle. He was struck in the head with a pipe and knocked unconscious.

Floyd Mann, head of the Alabama State Police, fired warning shots in the air to break up the mob. He ordered state police onto the scene and phoned Governor Patterson, who declared martial law in Montgomery. Robert Kennedy was furious that Governor Patterson had broken his promise to protect the riders. President John F. Kennedy sent U.S. marshals to Montgomery to ensure the riders were not attacked again.

National and international news focused on the Freedom Riders. Dr. Martin Luther King Jr. flew into Montgomery and held a rally at Ralph Abernathy's First Baptist Church to support them. U.S. marshals surrounded the church, but by nightfall, several thousand angry whites had gathered, making it impossible for those inside to leave safely. At 3 A.M., with the demonstrators still unable to leave the church, King angrily called Robert Kennedy to ask if law and order existed in America.

The mob hurled insults and bottles. The marshals threw tear gas, which drifted into the church and choked those inside. Kennedy demanded that the governor send in the state police and the Alabama National Guard to disperse the mob.

Fearing the growing violence, Kennedy asked King to talk the Freedom Riders into a "cooling off" period. In response, CORE's national director, James Farmer, said that blacks had been "cooling off for 350 years. . . . If we cooled off any more, we'd be in a deep freeze." The Freedom Riders decided to proceed on to Mississippi, where the roads had been lined with troops from the Mississippi National Guard.

There was no mob at the Jackson, Mississippi, station when the Freedom Riders arrived. The police simply walked them through the "whites only" section of the terminal and took them to jail. The riders were tried on May 25 and sentenced to sixty days in the state penitentiary. More volunteers poured into Jackson to take their place, and they were also arrested and put in jail.

By summer's end, more than three hundred Freedom Riders had been arrested. None ever made it to New Orleans, and many spent their summer behind bars. Still, the Freedom Rides of 1961 accomplished their goals. In 1961, at Robert Kennedy's request, the federal Interstate Commerce Commission banned segregation on interstate bus travel. Through their organized and nonviolent efforts, the Freedom Riders also shone a spotlight on the racist practices of the South and gained support for the American civil rights movement throughout the world.

FREEDOM SUMMER

(1964)

Is this America, the land of the free and the home of the brave, where we have to sleep with our telephones off the hooks because our lives be threatened daily, because we want to live as decent human beings, in America?
—*Fannie Lou Hamer, speaking to the Democratic National Convention, 1964*

The summer of 1964 is known as Freedom Summer. During that time, white and black students joined together in a series of actions designed to end discrimination in the South. Many of the most important people of the civil rights movement organized successful protests and activities during that summer.

Robert Moses of the Student Nonviolent Coordinating Committee (SNCC) designed

A Freedom Summer student volunteer encourages a black mother to vote.

the plan for Freedom Summer. Inspired by the success of the Freedom Vote, which taught tens of thousands of blacks in Mississippi how to cast ballots, Moses wanted to return to Mississippi. He wanted to lead a voter registration drive before the presidential elections in the fall.

Moses believed the participation of white volunteers from the North would draw attention to the problems that blacks faced in Mississippi. Others in the SNCC believed the Southerners should organize and direct their own activities.

Moses decided to end the debate and proceed on his own. He began to ask for volunteers from colleges in the North. More than a thousand students traveled to Western Women's College in Oxford, Ohio, for training. The mostly white volunteers were wealthy, and they had to bring five hundred dollars for bail and enough money for living expenses, medical bills, and their transportation home.

SNCC leader James Forman made sure the students understood the dangers they would face in Mississippi. He told them they had to be prepared to go to jail, be beaten, or even possibly be killed. If they weren't, they needed to go home.

He also gave them some rules for survival. For example, they could not appear together in interracial groups. Whoever was in the minority had to hide under a blanket or under floorboards. Forman also warned them to "go quietly to jail if arrested," for their own safety. "Mississippi is not the place to start conducting constitutional law classes for the policemen," he said.

Shortly after the first two hundred volunteers arrived in Mississippi, three SNCC workers disappeared—Michael Schwerner and Andrew Goodman, both white, and James Chaney, who was African American. The police claimed the disappearance was a publicity stunt intended to make the state look bad. Pictures of the three men and their story made the front page of newspapers across the country.

Despite the chilling disappearance of the three SNCC workers, very few volunteers were scared away. Instead, they became more determined. The rest of the one thousand volunteers arrived in the state. They set up Freedom Schools to teach reading and writing to black children. They encouraged people to register to vote and to join the newly formed Mississippi Freedom Democratic Party (MFDP).

Doctors from the Northeast arrived to set up Freedom Clinics, where African Americans could receive free and regular medical exams and treatment. The American Lawyers Guild, the American Jewish Committee, the NAACP Legal Defense and Educational Fund, and a host of law students held legal clinics to ensure that African Americans knew and claimed their basic rights.

Six weeks later, the bodies of the three missing men were found near Philadelphia, Mississippi. Segregationists made no apologies. State Congressman Arthur Winstead said, "When people leave any section of the country and go into another section looking for trouble they usually find it." The Federal Bureau of Investigation (FBI) arrested twenty-one men in connection with the murders, including Deputy Sheriff Cecil Price. Price had pulled the three men over for speeding shortly before their disappearance. Only six men were sent to jail for "civil rights violations." No one was jailed for murder.

One of the most important goals of Freedom Summer was to have delegates from the new party, the MFDP, at the 1964 Democratic National Convention in Atlantic City, New Jersey. The delegates hoped to unseat the all-white Mississippi delegation on the grounds that it did not represent the people of the state. The MFDP had four white delegates and sixty-four African American delegates, who represented the 850,000 unregistered African American voters in the state of Mississippi.

In August, MFDP leaders Fannie Lou Hamer, Aaron Henry, Victoria Gray, Ed King, and Annie Devine arrived at the convention. They spoke

Civil rights demonstrators at the 1964 Democratic National Convention

on national television about the unlawful Jim Crow laws and the abuse of African Americans who tried to vote.

The MFDP received support from other states, forcing President Lyndon B. Johnson to consider their request for a seat at the convention. Johnson was not willing to alienate his supporters, however. He did not want to lose the Democratic nomination for reelection. Johnson sent Senator Hubert Humphrey, his intended vice presidential running mate, to offer a compromise. Humphrey offered the MFDP two seats on the floor and promised that an all-white delegation would never again represent Mississippi.

The MFDP delegates refused to accept the offer—despite the urging of leaders Martin Luther King, Bayard Rustin, and Roy Wilkins to take it. The delegates had sacrificed their well-being, the safety of their families, their homes, and jobs to travel to Atlantic City to stand up for their beliefs. They would not accept anything less than what the U.S. Constitution guaranteed. The MFDP rejected Humphrey's compromise, but the rest of the convention voted to accept it. Moses, Hamer, and the others were disillusioned—but their efforts were not wasted.

Many believe that Freedom Summer changed the people who participated in it more than it changed the state of Mississippi. "I think that every time we got someone to register to vote—to attempt to register to vote, whether they were successful or not . . . every time we got someone to stand up and say, 'Yes, I'm going to the mass meeting,' we had changed them. You don't do that and then undo it two weeks later, and go back to what you were before that act," said Mississippi native Lawrence Guyot.

The Freedom Summer project was a training ground for activists who went on to lead the free speech, antiwar, and women's movements of the 1960s and 1970s. Many of the Mississippi activists remained in their home state to improve living conditions for people living in poverty and oppression. Mississippi now has more elected African American officials than any other state in the country.

FROM SELMA TO MONTGOMERY: MARCHING FOR THE VOTE

(1965)

The vote is the most powerful instrument ever devised by man for breaking down injustice and destroying the terrible walls which imprison men because they are different from other men.
—*President Lyndon B. Johnson*

The historic march from Selma, Alabama, to the state capitol in Montgomery led to the passage of the 1965 Voting Rights Act. Although the march took place in 1965, it really began in 1963. In February of that year, volunteers working for the Student Nonviolent Coordinating Committee (SNCC) held voting clinics in Selma to teach blacks how to exercise their right to vote. Two years later, twenty-five thousand African Americans marched to Montgomery to protect that right.

In the early 1960s, African Americans made up about half of the voting population in Selma, but only 1 percent were actually registered to vote. Jim Crow laws and the threat of abuse and violence made it difficult for blacks to register.

Dr. Martin Luther King Jr. arrived in Selma on January 2, 1965. He spoke to a crowd of seven hundred at Brown Chapel African Methodist Episcopal Church. He encouraged them to march to the courthouse together to register the next time the two-day voter registration was held.

Dr. King led the march to the courthouse on January 18 and 19. Sixty of the marchers were arrested. When Sheriff Jim Clark pushed Amelia Boynton, a teacher and registered voter, on the front steps of the courthouse, the press spread the pictures and the story across the nation.

Two days later, one hundred black teachers joined the demonstrations in protest of Boynton's arrest and mistreatment. On February 1, Dr. King was arrested. In response, hundreds of schoolchildren marched to the courthouse. Sheriff Clark made so many arrests, the jails were overflowing. Confrontations escalated.

On February 18, during a protest in Marion, Alabama, twenty-six-year-old Jimmie Lee Jackson was shot and killed by police as he tried to protect his mother and grandfather from being beaten by officers. Dozens of protesters and a reporter for NBC News were also brutally beaten.

When Rev. James Bevel heard the news, he suggested to Dr. King that the protesters march to confront Governor George Wallace in the capital city of Montgomery, more than 50 miles (80.5 km) away. Bevel was a member of the Southern Christian Leadership Conference (SCLC), which King led. The march was scheduled for March 7, 1965. Governor Wallace said in a press conference that he would not allow the march to take place because it would create a traffic jam along the highway.

On the morning of March 7, as six hundred marchers left Selma and crossed the Edmund Pettus Bridge, they were stopped by two hundred Alabama state troopers and sheriff's deputies, some on horseback. Major John Cloud ordered the marchers to turn back and gave them two minutes to comply.

Hosea Williams, the leader of the march, asked the major if the group could have a moment to pray. The marchers got down on their knees, and as Williams led them in prayer, Cloud gave the order to attack.

Sheyann Webb, who was eight years old at the time, remembered the scene long after. "All I could see was the outburst of tear gas. I saw people being beaten and I tried to run home as fast as I could. . . . Hosea Williams picked me up and I told him to put me down, he wasn't running fast enough."

Television stations interrupted their regular programming to show footage of the police beating and trampling the helpless marchers. The incident on Pettus Bridge became known as Bloody Sunday.

King sent telegrams to prominent clergy across America and invited them to Selma for a ministers' march two days later. Hundreds agreed to come, but this time the court stopped the march. The SCLC had asked a federal judge, Frank M. Johnson, to bar Governor Wallace from interfering with the march. Instead, the judge halted the march until he could hear both sides of the issue.

While waiting for the hearing date, three white Unitarian ministers were attacked while leaving a soul-food restaurant. One of them, James Reeb, died from his injuries.

On March 11, Judge Johnson listened to Dr. King and Sheriff Clark speak, but the judge did not issue a decision. Tension was high in the city. On March 15, President Lyndon B. Johnson gave a televised address to Congress and announced his new voting rights legislation. "Their cause must be our cause, too," the president said. "Because it's not just Negroes, but it's really all of us who must overcome the crippling legacy of bigotry and injustice. And we shall overcome."

Segregationists and activists alike were shocked that the president ended his speech with the slogan of the civil rights movement: "We shall overcome."

Later that night, Judge Johnson ruled that the activists had "a legal and constitutional right to march from Selma to Montgomery."

On March 21, 1965, hundreds gathered with Dr. King at Brown Chapel in Selma for the 54-mile (87-km) trek to Montgomery. The marchers pitched tents along the road at night. Teams of volunteers brought them food and water from headquarters in Selma. By the time the marchers arrived in Montgomery, their numbers had swelled to twenty-five thousand.

For their safety, the marchers were advised to leave Montgomery as soon as possible. Viola Liuzzo, a white woman from Detroit, Michigan, was one of the many who volunteered to drive the marchers back to Selma. She dropped off one group and headed back to Montgomery to pick up another. Her fifteen-year-old son, Leroy Moton, was with her. Ku Klux Klansmen spotted them on the road and chased them down Route 80. They pulled alongside her car, shot her twice, and killed her. After the car crashed into a ditch, the four men stopped to inspect the wreckage. Leroy Moton pretended to be dead, which saved his life. By noon the next day, the Klansmen were arrested.

President Johnson signed the Voting Rights Act into law on August 6, 1965. Thousands of African Americans living in the South registered to vote. By 1984, African Americans served as mayors in 255 cities.

THE MARTYRS OF THE ORANGEBURG MASSACRE

HENRY SMITH, SAMUEL HAMMOND JR.,
DELANO MIDDLETON, AND CLEVELAND SELLERS
(1968)

Truth crushed to the ground will still rise up.
—Cleveland Sellers

Cleveland Sellers in 2003

The Orangeburg Massacre took place in February 1968, just a few months before the assassination of Dr. Martin Luther King Jr. This little-known event was one of the most controversial incidents of brutality against African American students in America's history.

Orangeburg, South Carolina, was a college town, home to the historically black South Carolina State College and Claflin College. The only bowling alley in Orangeburg refused to integrate. On February 5, 1968, a courageous group of students led a demonstration to protest the segregation. The protest began peacefully but ended in violence. One officer and nine students went to the hospital. Others were treated at the state college infirmary. During the two days following the event, tensions continued to escalate.

On the cold night of February 8, a group of about a hundred students from the two colleges in town built a bonfire in front of the South Carolina State College campus. Firefighters were called to put out the flames, accompanied by an all-white team of state troopers. As the students left the scene to return to their campuses, someone tossed a banister rail, which hit a state trooper in the face.

Within minutes, seventy state police officers lined the South Carolina State campus, armed with carbines, pistols, and riot guns. Riot guns, which were often used to break up crowds, typically carried pellets too small to cause physical harm. That night, the weapons were loaded with enough buckshot to kill a deer, or a person.

A policeman fired his carbine into the air, reportedly as a warning shot, but the sound prompted the other officers to start shooting. The twenty-seven students injured had been retreating, so they were shot in their backs, sides, and the soles of their feet. Three students were killed: Henry Smith, nineteen, a Reserve Officers' Training Corps (ROTC) student; Samuel Hammond Jr., nineteen, a freshman halfback; and DeLano Middleton, seventeen, a high school football and baseball star, whose mother worked as a maid at the college.

The next day, South Carolina governor Robert McNair called a press conference. He blamed "black power advocates" for the violence. At that time, Stokely Carmichael's phrase "black power" was linked to the changing civil rights movement, which was moving away from nonviolent protest. The state troopers involved in the massacre described the students as a "threatening mob." They reported that students had charged the troopers, threw bricks, and fired small guns. No empty bullet cartridges were found in the area, however, and the only trooper injured had been hit by a piece of wood.

The National Guard marches in Orangeburg, South Carolina.

Nine of the police officers were charged with imposing punishment "without due process of the law"—but less than a year later, all the men were acquitted. Two and a half years later, Cleveland Sellers, the national program director for the Student Nonviolent Coordinating Committee (SNCC), was found guilty of rioting.

No one could place Sellers in the vicinity of the rioting on those two nights in February. His arrest was based on his alleged participation in the bowling-alley demonstration two nights before the shooting. Sellers was well known for his civil rights efforts in South Carolina and Mississippi. He was an organizer in SNCC's 1964 Freedom Summer project in Holly Springs, Mississippi. Sellers served seven months of a one-year sentence in state prison.

At the time, the Associated Press released an inaccurate account of the massacre, describing it as "a heavy exchange of gunfire." The true story got lost among the other tragedies that year, such as the assassination of Dr. King, the slaying of Robert F. Kennedy, and the violent protests against the Vietnam War at the Democratic National Convention in Chicago, Illinois.

In 1970, Jack Bass and Jack Nelson published their book *The Orangeburg Massacre*. Bass and Nelson are former reporters who covered the events as they unfolded. At the time, Bass was a reporter at the *Charlotte Observer* in North Carolina, and Nelson wrote for the *Los Angeles Times*. Many consider the book the definitive account of what really happened in Orangeburg.

Sellers was pardoned in 1993 and received an apology from South Carolina governor Carroll A. Campbell. Sellers has a master's degree from Harvard and a doctoral degree from the University of North Carolina at Greensboro. He is a professor of African American studies at the University of South Carolina. He has donated his papers to the College of Charleston's Avery Research Center for African American History and Culture.

The victims of the Orangeburg Massacre are honored in a course that is held as part of freshman orientation at South Carolina State College.

THE MEMPHIS SANITATION WORKERS' STRIKE

(1968)

I am a man!

In Memphis, Tennessee, in the 1960s, white workers in the Memphis Department of Sanitation operated the heavy machinery, and the African Americans picked up the trash. Although these African American workers performed one of the most important public-health jobs in the city, people in both white and black communities looked down on them. They were also paid a low wage and received no benefits, vacation, or pension. Even though they worked full-time, 40 percent of them qualified for welfare.

On February 1, 1968, Echol Cole and Robert Walker tried to take shelter from the rain in the back of their garbage truck, when an electric short triggered the compressor. The two men were crushed to death. The sanitation department had refused to update the workers' run-down vehicles, which led to the accident.

On February 12, sanitation workers decided to strike. Nine hundred thirty of the 1,100 sanitation workers went on strike. Street-repair crews also joined them. The American Federation of State, County and Municipal Employees sent Mayor Henry Loeb a telegram. It outlined the nine points

Memphis sanitation workers on strike in 1968

that the sanitation workers wanted the mayor to address. They wanted a union that would protect their rights; a method for formally submitting complaints; an increase in wages; and a system for promotions, pensions, insurance, and other benefits.

The National Association for the Advancement of Colored People (NAACP) sent a letter to the mayor in support of the sanitation workers' demands. The organization threatened to stage protests and launch a telephone campaign that would tie up the lines to city hall and the fire and police departments.

The sanitation workers appealed to African American councilman Fred Davis to help them. He said he would try to find a way to present the demands without alienating white council members. Davis told sanitation workers that the city council was planning to vote on the issue on February 23, so they canceled the sit-in they had been planning.

On the date of the vote, about fifteen hundred sanitation workers, union leaders, and ministers gathered at city hall to hear the results. When Davis announced that the council had approved a pay raise of only five cents per hour, the disappointed strikers accused Davis of betraying them. The council meeting ended immediately.

Community leaders suggested that the strikers march from city hall to the Mason Temple to express their frustration in a peaceful protest. The police gave their permission for the march to take place but instructed the marchers to walk on the right side of the street. The police followed them closely in vehicles, nudging the crowd. When a police cruiser ran over one woman's foot, the strikers began to push it. The police responded by spraying the crowd with Mace, which is a form of tear gas.

The next day, several community organizers—including civil rights leader Rev. James Lawson—formed the Community on the Move for Equality (COME). The group asked supporters to boycott downtown businesses, especially any connected to Mayor Loeb and his family. The strikers, carrying signs, marched in peaceful demonstrations every day.

"The sign that they carried during the strike didn't say, 'Peace,' didn't say, 'Freedom.' It didn't say, 'Justice.' It said, 'I am a man,'" said Rev. Samuel Billy Kyles of Monumental Baptist Church. In the South, adult African American men and women were referred to disrespectfully as boys and girls. The declaration "I Am a Man" cut to the core issue in this strike—respect. Support for the sanitation workers grew. High school youth, college students, and teachers marched alongside the sanitation workers, ministers, and community leaders.

Loeb hired new workers to pick up the trash, but there were so many men on strike, he couldn't hire enough to maintain the daily collection schedule. So the trash piled up. By February 14, there was more than ten thousand tons of garbage on the streets.

With each march, police hostility toward the protesters increased. White and African American ministers held nightly prayer vigils. On March 5,

Martin Luther King Jr. with leaders of the Memphis sanitation workers' strike

more than one hundred protesters were arrested. Still, the mayor would not negotiate. He insisted it was against the law for public workers to strike. Some discouraged workers returned to their jobs.

COME leaders contacted civil rights leaders across the country. On March 14, Roy Wilkins, president of the NAACP, and national labor leader Bayard Rustin spoke to a crowd of ten thousand at the Mason Temple. Andrew Young, Ralph Abernathy, Jesse Jackson, and many others leaders came to help, too. On March 18, Dr. Martin Luther King Jr. arrived to address more than thirteen thousand strikers and community supporters.

On March 28, Dr. King returned to Memphis to lead a march, but only minutes before the march was to begin, violence broke out. Six hundred police attacked the crowd with nightsticks and tear gas. Marchers broke windows and looted stores. That night, Tennessee declared martial law. There was a dusk-to-dawn curfew for African Americans. Some four thousand troops of the National Guard descended on the city in tanks.

Many people feared the nonviolent demonstrations of the civil rights movement had become a thing of the past. King was criticized for not being able to lead a peaceful protest. He returned to the city again in April to prove that he could.

On the night of April 3, in the midst of loud thunder, high winds, and the threat of a tornado, a large crowd gathered to hear Martin Luther King give his famous "Mountaintop" speech. "For when people get caught up with that which is right and they are willing to sacrifice for it, there is no stopping point short of victory," he told the crowd.

The next day, King was assassinated outside of his room at the Lorraine Motel. Hundreds of ministers rushed to Mayor Loeb's office to demand that he negotiate with the sanitation workers. He refused.

On April 8, 1968, King's hope for a peaceful march in Memphis was fulfilled. Police estimated there were nineteen thousand marchers, but Bayard Rustin confirmed a count of forty-two thousand. King's widow, Coretta Scott King, led the dignified marchers through the streets, urging them to keep her husband's spirit alive.

Leaders from across the country reached out to support the strike. The United Auto Workers pledged fifty thousand dollars to help the sanitation workers and vowed to fight Mayor Loeb. The mayor's colleagues accused him of ruining the city.

President Lyndon B. Johnson finally sent a negotiator from the U.S. Labor Department to help the city and the sanitation workers reach an agreement. On April 16, the sanitation workers and their supporters gathered at city hall again. This time, the city council voted in their favor. The sixty-five-day strike was over. Conditions soon improved for sanitation workers across America, and the civil rights movement had new leaders, new issues, and a new sense of power for the people.

RESURRECTION CITY AND THE POOR PEOPLE'S CAMPAIGN

(1968)

*What we now need is a new kind of Selma or Birmingham
to dramatize the economic plight of the Negro and compel the
government to act.*
—Martin Luther King Jr.

By 1967, the civil rights movement had created some change for the better—but conditions still had not improved enough. African Americans had suffered greatly and yet were still struggling to survive. Segregation and discrimination created economic inequalities for African Americans, including substandard housing, low-paying jobs, and unemployment.

People were enraged, and the violence was increasing. A string of urban riots broke out in seven major cities across the nation. Dr. Martin Luther King knew it was time for a new plan.

In November 1967, he met with the leaders of the Southern Christian Leadership Conference (SCLC) to plan a Poor People's Campaign. King believed his new plan was the second phase of the civil rights movement. The Poor People's Campaign would bring together all people in need—white, Native American, Puerto Rican, Mexican, and others. "The poor are no longer divided," he said.

King's plan was to assemble 1,500 protesters in Washington, D.C. The event would, he hoped, pressure Congress to pass a thirty billion dollar package that would provide full employment, a guaranteed annual income, and more low-income housing. King considered the package an "economic bill of rights."

On December 4, 1967, Dr. King held a press conference to announce his plan. He promised the campaign would be nonviolent but "strong, dramatic and attention getting." On April 4, 1968, while King was still finalizing his plans, a sniper's bullet ended his life. The SCLC vowed to carry out the fallen leader's last campaign. King's longtime friend, the Reverend Ralph Abernathy, became the new president of the organization.

The six-week-long campaign began on May 14. People from across the country came to the District of Columbia in caravans of cars, buses, trains, and even mule trains. The SCLC had organized nine caravans from different regions: the Eastern Caravan, the Appalachian Trail, the Southern Caravan, the Midwest Caravan, the Indian Trail, the San Francisco Caravan, the Western Caravan, the Mule Train, and the Freedom Train. Each caravan stopped in several cities along the way to pick up more people.

More than three thousand of America's poor arrived in the nation's capital. They built a temporary shantytown around the Lincoln Memorial. The settlement, which spread along fifteen acres of West Potomac Park, was named Resurrection City, U.S.A.

Resurrection City was a functional town, complete with its own zip code, a city hall, cultural center, dining tent, and medical dispensary. The U.S. Park

A muddy path in Resurrection City after a rainfall

Police were not allowed to enter, so Resurrection City maintained its own police force.

Conditions were severe, however. For twenty-eight of the forty days of the campaign, rain poured down on the city. *Washington Post* reporter Ben W. Gilbert described the scene in his book *Ten Blocks from the White House: An Anatomy of the Washington Riots of 1968:* "The grassy parkland turned to trampled mud, ankle deep, with some puddles of water hip deep. The plywood homes were soaked. . . . Trash, rotting food, discarded clothing, packing boxes, cans, and liquor bottles slowly sank into the mud throughout the encampment."

June 19 was Solidarity Day, and some 50,000 people from all over the country came to the nation's capital to join the march. Soon after the event, however, the population of Resurrection City dropped to 300. Many of those who stayed had no money and nowhere else to go. Tensions grew between city officials and the protesters. After two days of riots—during which some 1,000 police officers released police dogs and tear gas—Resurrection City was closed. More than 150 people were arrested, including Rev. Abernathy.

The civil rights movement—the era of nonviolent protest and grassroots organization—was over. Although it had gained many significant victories despite bitter opposition, the movement fell short of achieving its ultimate goal: the equality and freedom of all Americans. The movement did, however, open the door for many new movements—the antiwar movement, the women's movement, the gay rights movement, and others. The American civil rights movement helped people see that the struggle of each one of us is the struggle for all of us.

I think it's really important that young people today understand that the movement of the sixties was really a people's movement . . . that it was people just like them, their age, that formulated goals and strategies, and actually developed the movement. When they look around now, and see things that need to be changed, they should say: "What can I do? What can my roommate and I do to effect that change?"
—Diane Nash, chairman of the central committee, Nashville Student Movement

MORE EXTRAORDINARY PEOPLE OF THE CIVIL RIGHTS MOVEMENT

Victoria Gray Adams and Annie Devine

Adams and Devine were Mississippi businesswomen and cofounders, with Fannie Lou Hamer, of the Mississippi Freedom Democratic Party. At a time when many African Americans were leaving Mississippi, Adams said, "I'm choosing to stay here and fight for the opportunity to be able to live in Mississippi as well as I can anywhere else." Adams, Devine, and Hamer were the first African American women to be seated on the House floor. They exposed election abuses and Jim Crow practices in their home state.

Dr. William G. Anderson

Anderson was elected president of the Albany Movement of Albany, Georgia. A former classmate of Dr. Martin Luther King Jr., Anderson called his old friend and asked him to speak at a mass meeting. After King arrived, Anderson convinced the prominent civil rights leader to remain in town to lead the march, which put the Albany Movement in the national spotlight.

L. Roy Bennett

This minister and civil rights activist was president of the Interdenominational Ministerial Alliance (IMA). Jo Ann Robinson approached the IMA to ask its support for the Montgomery Bus Boycott. Bennett strongly urged the ministers to participate.

Randolph Blackwell

Blackwell was a lawyer and college professor. In 1962, he joined the staff of the Southern Christian Leadership Conference (SCLC) to work for the Voter Education Project. A year later, he became field director of the project, serving through some of the most bitterly contested voting rights campaigns in the South. In 1964, he was appointed program director of the SCLC, a position he held until July 1964, when he left to found Southern Rural Action, Inc.

Flonzie Goodloe Brown-Wright

Because of Jim Crow laws in Mississippi, African Americans had to pass strict tests before they could register to vote. When Brown-Wright tried to register, the registrar asked her to define the legal term *habeas corpus.* She had no idea what it meant, so she failed the test. She returned home to study the Mississippi Constitution, and the next time she took the test, she passed it easily. She vowed to someday get the job of the man who denied her the right to vote, which she did. In 1968, Brown-Wright became election commissioner—and the first black woman to be elected to hold public office in Mississippi.

C. Curtis Bryant

Bryant was head of the local chapter of the National Association for the Advancement of Colored People in McComb, Mississippi. He led sit-ins and demonstrations and worked with Robert "Bob" Moses of the Student Nonviolent Coordinating Committee to set up a voter registration project in the area.

John Michael Doar

Doar was a federal prosecutor for the civil rights division of the U.S. Justice Department. He worked on behalf of James Meredith in 1962, during Meredith's attempt to register at the University of Mississippi. After the death of civil rights activist Medgar Evers, Doar placed himself between angry African-American youth and police to prevent rioting. He also prosecuted the men accused of lynching Michael Schwerner, Andrew Goodman, and James Chaney, the three volunteers who traveled to Mississippi from the North to register voters during the 1964 Freedom Summer. The events of the trial were later made into a movie called *Mississippi Burning*.

A. G. Gaston

Gaston was an African American millionaire in Birmingham, Alabama, and a supporter of the civil rights movement. He hosted Southern Christian Leadership Conference members at a motel he owned during the Birmingham demonstrations.

Tom Hayden

Hayden was a Freedom Rider and an important figure in the student movement of the 1960s. He was one of the founders of the Students for a Democratic Society, a Northern-based organization of mainly white students who supported the civil rights movement. In 1964, he worked in Newark, New Jersey, as a community organizer to create a national poor people's campaign for jobs and economic power.

Esau Jenkins

In the 1950s, Jenkins was a bus driver on a route from Johns Island to Charleston, South Carolina. While attending a workshop at the Highlander Folk School, he shared the story of the people on his bus who asked him to teach them to read and write. These passengers wanted to study the U.S. Constitution so they could pass the literacy test required when registering to vote. Jenkins's story inspired Septima Poinsette Clark to establish the first citizenship school on Johns Island.

Samuel "Billy" Kyles

Rev. Kyles was a leader in the civil rights movement in Memphis, Tennessee. After Memphis sanitation workers went on strike in February 1968, he convinced Dr. Martin Luther King Jr. to come to Memphis to speak with them. Kyles led nightly rallies to raise money for the protesters. He was with King when the civil rights leader was assassinated at the Lorraine Motel in Memphis on April 4, 1968. Kyles is the pastor of Monumental Baptist Church in Memphis.

Autherine Lucy

Two years before the 1954 U.S. Supreme Court ruling in *Brown v. Board of Education,* Lucy was accepted to the historically all-white University of Alabama. When the school discovered she was African American, it did not allow her to attend. In 1956, she again tried to attend the school but was confronted by mobs of students, townspeople, and out-of-state segregationists. Lucy was suspended from the school for her own safety. More than thirty years later, she enrolled in the university to get her master's degree in elementary education. Her daughter enrolled in the school at around the same time. Mother and daughter graduated together in 1992.

Charles "Chuck" McDrew

McDrew was a student organizer for the Student Nonviolent Coordinating Committee. During the Freedom Summer of 1964, he and civil rights activist Robert Moses started a Nonviolent High School to train young protesters in nonviolent methods of creating social change. When the white community learned about the school, Moses and McDrew were arrested and spent four months in a Mississippi jail.

Floyd McKissick

McKissick was a skilled attorney and businessman and a champion of civil rights. He was the first African American to study at the University of North Carolina Law School at Chapel Hill. He served as national chairman of the Congress of Racial Equality and later replaced James Farmer as its national director. McKissick also held an advisory role with the National Association for the Advancement of Colored People and was the founder and president of McKissick Enterprises. In the early 1970s, he founded Soul City near Warrenton, North Carolina—a new township designed to financially empower African Americans.

Chris McNair

Photographer Chris McNair has documented some of the most controversial moments in Alabama's history. He photographed Governor George Wallace when he made his notorious stand against integration by blocking the door at the University of Alabama to keep black students from entering. McNair's most memorable photo is of the damage caused by the 1963 bombing of the Sixteenth Street Baptist Church in Birmingham. The blast killed four young girls, including the photographer's daughter, eleven-year-old Denise.

Sidna Brower Mitchell

Mitchell was the editor of the *Daily Mississippian,* the campus paper of the University of Mississippi. In 1962, she wrote an editorial that called for her fellow students to end the riots protesting the admission of James Meredith, the college's first African American student. The student senate censured her for what they saw as disloyalty to the Southern way of life. She was later nominated for a Pulitzer Prize for the editorials she wrote during the crisis.

Joan Mulholland

Mulholland was a white civil rights activist in Mississippi. She attended the historically black Tougaloo College. She did not believe that integration meant only that African Americans should be allowed to enter white society; she believed that whites should also be allowed into African American society. Mulholland was a Virginia native and an active member of the Student Nonviolent Coordinating Committee. She participated in the first student sit-in at the Woolworth's lunch counter in Jackson, Mississippi, and spent a summer in the Hines County jail for her civil rights activities.

Joseph L. Rauh Jr.

Rauh was a white lawyer who was active in the liberal wing of the national Democratic Party. He volunteered his services as counsel for the Mississippi Freedom Democratic Party (MFDP) at the 1964 Democratic National Convention in Atlantic City, New Jersey. The MFDP sought to unseat the all-white Mississippi delegation, which did not fairly represent the largely black population of the state. Rauh was also general counsel to the Leadership Conference on Civil Rights. He worked with Clarence Mitchell to lobby for several Voting Rights Acts (1965, 1970, and 1975), the Fair Housing Act of 1968, and other civil rights legislation.

Amelia Boynton Robinson

In 1964, Robinson became the first female African American ever to seek a seat in Congress from Alabama—and the first woman of any race to run on the Democratic Party ticket in the state. She participated in the 1965 Selma march and the event known as Bloody Sunday. The image of her lying on the Edmund Pettus Bridge was published in newspapers around the world. Robinson's home in Selma was a meeting place and planning center for civil rights leaders. She was an invited guest of honor when President Lyndon B. Johnson signed the Voting Rights Act in 1965.

Bernice Robinson

Robinson was a teacher in the first citizenship school, which was on Johns Island, South Carolina. She was employed by both the Highlander Folk School and the Southern Christian Leadership Conference (SCLC) to set up voter registration workshops in communities across the South. Robinson waged the most successful literacy campaign in the United States. She left the SCLC in 1970 and went to work with the South Carolina Commission for Farm Workers (SCCFW). In 1972 she made an unsuccessful bid for Congress. She returned to the SCCFW and continued to work with migrant farmworkers until 1977.

Charles Sherrod

Sherrod was among the first field workers for the Student Nonviolent Coordinating Committee to arrive in Albany, Georgia. His efforts, along with the work of other civil rights activists from the Youth Council of the National Association for the Advancement of Colored People, brought about the establishment of the Albany Movement in 1961. Sherrod was elected to the city commission of Albany in 1971.

Constance Iona Slaughter-Harvey

Slaughter-Harvey was the first African American woman to graduate from the University of Mississippi Law School and to integrate the Mississippi Bar Association. During her studies at the law school, she endured the racism and sexism of the all-white, all-male law students. She went on to become assistant secretary of state in Mississippi. In 1978, President Jimmy Carter appointed her to the Presidential Scholars Commission.

Kelly Miller Smith Sr.

An activist in the civil rights movement in Tennessee, Smith served as president of several organizations, including the Opportunities and Industrialized Center, the National Conference of Black Churchmen, the Nashville Christian Leadership Conference (which he founded), and the Nashville chapter of the National Association for the Advancement of Colored People. Smith served as assistant dean of the Divinity School of Vanderbilt University in Nashville from 1970 until 1984.

Maxine Smith

Smith was the executive secretary of the Memphis, Tennessee, chapter of the National Association for the Advancement of Colored People. She organized the "If You're Black, Take It Back" boycott of downtown stores that refused to integrate. In 1961, she escorted thirteen first-graders to four historically white public schools. Protesting the city schools' ongoing refusal to integrate, Smith helped coordinated Black Mondays, during which African American students, teachers, and principals stayed home from school. This tactic caused the school board to restructure and opened the door for African Americans to be elected to the Memphis school board. By 1971, Smith won a seat on the Memphis City School Board of Education and later served as commissioner. She also served on the board of the National Civil Rights Museum of Memphis.

Maurice Sorrell

Sorrell captured images of the civil rights movement from the early days of Jim Crow segregation to the 1965 march from Selma to Montgomery, Alabama. The award-winning photographer later worked as a photojournalist for *Jet* and *Ebony* magazines. He was the first African American member of the White House Photographers Association.

Wyatt T. Walker

Walker was at the helm of the civil rights movement in Virginia and became executive director of the Southern Christian Leadership Conference (SCLC). He was also the Petersburg branch president for the National Association for the Advancement of Colored People and state director of the Congress of Racial Equality. Walker headed the Petersburg Improvement Association and legally forced integration of the Petersburg public library. He helped organize the Freedom Rides of 1960 and 1961 and was essential in the development of Project C, which laid the foundation for the demonstrations in Birmingham, Alabama, in 1963. In 1964, Walker became vice president of Educational Heritage, a publishing firm in Yonkers, New York, while continuing to serve on the SCLC board of directors.

Marian Wright-Edelman

Wright-Edelman graduated from Spelman College and Yale Law School. She was the first African American woman to practice law in Mississippi. She worked on voter registration drives in that state and worked for the Legal Defense and Educational Fund of the National Association for the Advancement of Colored People. In l968, she was counsel for Dr. Martin Luther King Jr.'s Poor People's Campaign. In 1973, she founded the Children's Defense Fund to address the needs of poor, minority, and handicapped children.

GLOSSARY

activist: a person who takes direct action to support or oppose an issue or belief.

apartheid: the government policy of segregation, or separation, of the races, in the Republic of South Africa from 1948 to 1994, when Nelson Mandela was elected president in the country's first democratic election.

Black Nationalism: the idea that black people should not integrate into white society but should be a separate and self-sufficient society.

black power: a term coined by civil rights activist Stokely Carmichael, which became a call for African Americans to unite for cultural and political power.

blacklisted: to be placed on a list of people to be punished or boycotted because of their ideas or beliefs.

boycott: to refuse to have dealings with a person, business, or organization in order to express disapproval or force change.

civil rights: the legal rights of personal liberty that belong to all citizens in American society, as guaranteed by the U.S. Constitution.

COFO: the Council of Federated Organizations, founded in 1961, to bring together several small and large civil rights organizations—including the SNCC, NAACP, and CORE—to focus on voter registration.

communism: a political system in which the government owns all the land and businesses, and the profits are shared by the people according to need.

Communist: A person who is a member of the Communist party, which supports the political idea of communism.

conscientious objector: a person who refuses to serve in the military or go to war because of religious or personal objections to war and violence.

CORE: the Congress of Racial Equality, a sister organization of FOR, founded in 1942 by Bernice Fisher, James Farmer, and others to organize and lead boycotts, sit-ins, marches, and other forms of nonviolent protest.

curfew: a rule that requires businesses to close and people to vacate town or city streets by a specific hour of the day.

draft: the selection of a person by the government for required military service.

five-and-ten store: a type of department store popular in the early twentieth century that sold most articles for five or ten cents; also known as five-and-dimes.

FOR: Fellowship of Reconciliation, founded in 1914 as an antiwar organization, which supported the idea of nonviolent action as a method of creating social change.

Freedom Rides: a series of protests against segregation on interstate travel, staged by black and white activists traveling by bus through the southern United States.

Freedom Schools: schools established in the South during the civil rights movement to teach African American children confidence, political organization skills, and voter literacy.

G.I. Bill of Rights: a government law providing veterans returning from World War II with tuition for college or vocational education and a year's pay.

grassroots: describes an organization or activity that operates on a small scale and encourages ordinary people to work together to find solutions to their own problems. It can also refer to networks of local communities that band together to address shared social issues.

Head Start: a government program started in 1965 to meet the health, educational, and psychological needs of preschool children in low-income families.

Jim Crow laws: discriminatory practices developed in the 1880s in the southern United States to restrict the personal liberties and rights of African Americans.

Ku Klux Klan: a secret society of white supremacists, founded after the Civil War, which opposed desegregation in the South and other civil rights for African Americans.

lobbyist: a person who works to influence politicians to support or oppose a specific issue.

martial law: the temporary enforcement of law by military forces rather than civilian forces during an emergency.

martyr: a person who sacrifices something of value, or life itself, for a belief or principle.

MIA: the Montgomery Improvement Association, founded in 1955 to organize the bus boycott in Montgomery, Alabama, which led to the U.S. Supreme Court ruling that outlawed segregated seating on public buses.

militant: a person who is aggressive in asserting an idea or belief.

NAACP: the National Association for the Advancement of Colored People, established in 1909 to protect the rights of African Americans and to work toward eliminating racial discrimination.

pacifist: a person who is opposed to war and violence.

peace church: one of several religious organizations, such as the Quaker church, that actively oppose war and violence.

picket: a demonstration of people positioned in a particular location, usually in front of a business or government building, to support or oppose an action or idea.

poll taxes: fixed amounts of money that new voters had to pay to the state in order to exercise the right to vote.

precedent: a legal case that establishes a principle or rule that is referred to when a court hears a later case with similar issues or facts.

Quaker: a person who is a member of the Quaker church, a Christian church that opposes war and is also known as the Religious Society of Friends.

Reconstruction: the period following the Civil War during which the Confederate states of the South were under the control of the federal government and the system of slavery was abolished.

SCLC: the Southern Christian Leadership Conference, an organization of ministers and other church leaders committed to working for civil rights, which was founded in 1957 and led by Dr. Martin Luther King Jr.

segregation: the legal separation of the races in public institutions and in society.

sharecropper: a farmer in the South who worked the land on a plantation in exchange for a share of the crop value.

sit-in: the act of sitting in a particular location and refusing to move as a means of protest.

SNCC: the Student Nonviolent Coordinating Committee, established in 1960 under the direction of Ella Baker, to organize students in nonviolent direct protest against segregation and racism.

socialist: one who believes in a political and economic system in which property and resources are owned by all the members of a society rather than by individuals or private businesses.

white supremacist: a person who believes that the white race is superior to all others and who treats people of other races with hostility.

TO FIND OUT MORE

BOOKS FOR YOUNG READERS

Adler, David, and Robert Casilla (illustrator). *A Picture Book of Martin Luther King Jr.* New York: Holiday House, 1989.

Ball, Howard, Dale Krane, and Thomas P. Lauth. *Compromised Compliance: Implementation of the 1965 Voting Rights Act.* Westport, Conn.: Greenwood Press, 1982.

Coles, Robert, and George Ford (illustrator). *The Story of Ruby Bridges.* New York: Scholastic, 1995.

Farris, Christine King, and Chris Soentpiet (illustrator). *My Brother Martin: A Sister Remembers Growing Up with the Reverend Dr. Martin Luther King Jr.* New York: Simon & Schuster Books for Young Readers, 2003.

Graves, Kerry A. *I Have a Dream: The Story behind Martin Luther King Jr.'s Most Famous Speech.* Philadelphia: Chelsea Clubhouse, 2004.

Haskins, James. *Freedom Rides: Journey for Justice.* New York: Hyperion Books for Children, 1995.

Haskins, James. *I Have A Dream: The Life and Words of Martin Luther King Jr.* Brookfield, Conn.: Millbrook Press, 1992.

King, Casey, and Linda Barrett Osborne. *Oh, Freedom! Kids Talk about the Civil Rights Movement with the People Who Made It Happen.* New York: Knopf, 1997.

King, Martin Luther. *I Have a Dream.* New York: Scholastic, 1997.

Lucas, Eileen, and Mark Anthony (illustrator). *Cracking the Wall: The Struggles of the Little Rock Nine.* Minneapolis: Carolrhoda Books, 1997.

Marzollo, Jean, and J. Brian Pinkney (illustrator). *Happy Birthday, Martin Luther King.* New York: Scholastic, 1993.

McNatt, Rosemary Bray. *Martin Luther King.* New York: Greenwillow, 1995.

Medaris, Angela Shelf, and Ann Rich (illustrator). *Dare to Dream: Coretta Scott King and the Civil Rights Movement.* New York: Lodestar Books, 1994.

Miller, Jake. *The 1963 March on Washington: Speeches and Songs for Civil Rights.* New York: PowerKids Press, 2004.

Miller, Jake. *The March from Selma to Montgomery: African Americans Demand the Vote.* New York: PowerKids Press, 2004.

Miller, Jake. *Sit-Ins and Freedom Rides: The Power of Nonviolent Resistance.* New York: PowerKids Press, 2004.

Moore, Yvette. *Freedom Songs.* New York: Puffin Books, 1992.

Price Hossell, Karen. *I Have a Dream.* Chicago: Heinemann, 2006.

Rappaport, Doreen, and Bryan Collier (illustrator). *Martin's Big Words: The Life of Dr. Martin Luther King Jr.* New York: Hyperion Books for Children, 2001.

Ribeiro, Myra. *Assassination of Medgar Evers.* New York: Rosen Publishing Group, 2002.

Ringgold, Faith. *If a Bus Could Talk: The Story of Rosa Parks.* New York: Simon & Schuster Books for Young People, 1999.

Ringgold, Faith. *My Dream of Martin Luther King.* New York: Crown, 1995.

Ruffin, Frances E., and Stephen Marchesi (illustrator). *Martin Luther King Jr. and the March on Washington.* New York: Grosset & Dunlap, 2001.

Weatherford, Carole Boston, and Jerome Lagarrigue (illustrator). *Freedom on the Menu: The Greensboro Sit-Ins.* New York: Dial Books for Young Readers, 2005.

Webb, Sheyann, and Rachel West Nelson. *Selma, Lord, Selma.* University of Alabama Press, 1980.

Wiles, Deborah, and Jerome Lagarrigue (illustrator). *Freedom Summer.* New York: Atheneum Books for Young Readers, 2001.

BOOKS FOR OLDER READERS (GRADES 4 AND UP)

Allen, Zita. *Black Women Leaders of the Civil Rights Movement.* Danbury, Conn.: Franklin Watts, 1996.

Andryszewski, Tricia. *March on Washington, 1963: Gathering to Be Heard.* Brookfield, Conn.: Millbrook Press, 1996.

Archer, Jules. *They Had a Dream: The Civil Rights Struggle from Frederick Douglass to Marcus Garvey to Martin Luther King and Malcolm X.* New York: Viking Books, 1993.

Coleman, Evelyn. *Circle of Fire.* Middleton, Wis.: Pleasant Company Publications, 2001.

Crewe, Sabrina, and Scott Ingram. *The 1963 Civil Rights March.* Milwaukee: Gareth Stevens, 2005.

Dallard, Shyrlee. *Ella Baker: A Leader behind the Scenes.* Englewood Cliffs, N.J.: Silver Burdett Press, 1990.

Davis, Ossie. *Just Like Martin.* New York: Simon & Schuster Books for Young Readers, 1992.

Evers-Williams, Myrlie. *For Us, the Living.* Jackson, Miss.: Banner Books, 1996.

Finlayson, Reggie. *We Shall Overcome: The History of the American Civil Rights Movement.* Minneapolis: Lerner Publishing Group, 2003.

Fradin, Judith Bloom, and Dennis Brindell Fradin. *The Power of One: Daisy Bates and the Little Rock Nine.* New York: Clarion Books, 2004.

Fremon, David K. *Jim Crow Laws and Racism in American History.* Berkeley Heights, N.J.: Enslow Publishers, 2000.

George, Linda, and Charles George. *Civil Rights Marches.* New York: Children's Press, 2000.

Kelso, Richard, and Mel Williges (illustrator). *Days of Courage: The Little Rock Story.* Austin, Tex.: Raintree Steck-Vaughn, 1993.

Koestler-Grack, Rachel A. *Going to School During the Civil Rights Movement.* Mankato, Minn.: Blue Earth Books, 2002.

Levine, Ellen. *Freedom's Children: Young Civil Rights Activists Tell Their Own Stories.* New York: Putnam, 1993.

Mayer, Robert H. (editor). *Civil Rights Act of 1964.* San Diego: Greenhaven Press, 2004.

McKissack, Pat. *Civil Rights Movement in America from 1865 to the Present.* Chicago: Children's Press, 1991.

McKissack, Patricia C., and Gordon C. James (illustrator). *Abby Takes a Stand.* New York: Viking Penguin, 2005.

Meltzer, Milton. *There Comes a Time: The Struggle for Civil Rights.* New York: Random House, 2001.

Miller, Marilyn. T*he Bridge at Selma: Turning Points in American History.* Morristown, N.J.: Silver Burdett Press, 1985.

Myers, Walter Dean. *Now Is Your Time! The African American Struggle for Freedom.* New York: HarperTrophy, 1991.

Parks, Rosa, and Jim Haskins. *Rosa Parks: My Story.* New York: Dial Books, 1992.

Pinkney, Andrea Davis, and Stephen Alcorn (illustrator). *Let It Shine: Stories of Black Women Freedom Fighters.* San Diego: Harcourt, 2000.

Powledge, Fred. *We Shall Overcome: Heroes of the Civil Rights Movement.* New York: Scribner, 1993.

Rochelle, Belinda. *Witnesses to Freedom: Young People Who Fought for Civil Rights.* New York: Dutton, 1993.

Thomas, Joyce Carol, and Curtis James (illustrator). *Linda Brown, You Are Not Alone: The Brown v. Board of Education Decision.* New York: Jump at the Sun/Hyperion Books for Children, 2003.

Tillage, Leon, and Susan Roth (illustrator). *Leon's Story.* New York: Farrar Straus Giroux, 1997.

Turck, Mary C. *Civil Rights Movement for Kids: A History with 21 Activities.* Chicago: Chicago Review Press, 2000.

Walter, Mildred Pitts. *Mississippi Challenge.* New York: Bradbury Press, 1992.

Weisbrot, Robert. *Marching toward Freedom 1957–1965: From the Founding of the Southern Christian Leadership Conference to the Assassination of Malcolm X.* New York: Chelsea House, 1994.

Wexler, Sanford. *Civil Rights Movement: An Eyewitness History.* New York: Facts on File, 1993.

Wilson, Camilla. *Rosa Parks: From the Back of the Bus to the Front of a Movement.* New York: Scholastic, 2001.

Selected Web Sites

About.com African American History

http://afroamhistory.about.com/

About.com provides a collection of primary texts, including the writings of famous African American leaders.

African American Odyssey

http://lcweb2.loc.gov/ammem/aaohtml/

A digital treasure chest from the Library of Congress (LOC), this section of the American Memory project includes highlights from the LOC's African American collections.

Birmingham Civil Rights Institute

http://www.bcri.org/index.html

Searchable database of manuscripts and oral histories.

Brown v. Board of Education

http://brownvboard.org/

Civil Rights Documentation Project

http://www.usm.edu/crdp/index.html

Civil Rights in Mississippi Digital Archive

http://www.lib.usm.edu/~spcol/crda/index.html
http://www.lib.usm.edu/%7Espcol/crda/index.html

Civil Rights Law and History

http://www.usdoj.gov/kidspage/crt/crtmenu.htm

Civil Rights Memorial

http://www.tolerance.org/memorial/

The Civil Rights Movement, 1955–1965

http://www.watson.org/~lisa/blackhistory/civilrights-55-65/

Civil Rights Oral History Interviews
http://www.wsulibs.wsu.edu/holland/masc/xcivilrights.html

FBI—Freedom of Information Act
http://foia.fbi.gov

Greensboro Sit-ins: Launch of a Civil Rights Movement
http://www.sitins.com/index.shtml

Historical Publications of the United States Commission on Civil Rights
http://www.law.umaryland.edu/edocs/usccr/html%20files/usccrhp.asp

Jim Crow Museum of Racist Memorabilia
http://www.ferris.edu/news/jimcrow/

The King Center
http://www.thekingcenter.com/

The Malcolm X Project at Columbia University
http://www.columbia.edu/cu/ccbh/mxp/

Malcolm X: A Research Site
http://www.brothermalcolm.net/

The Martin Luther King Jr. Papers Project
http://www.stanford.edu/group/King/

Mississippi Freedom Democratic Party
http://www.usm.edu/crdp/html/cd/mfdp.htm#audio#audio
Aaron Henry explains why the Mississippi Freedom Democratic Party refused the two seats offered at the 1964 Democratic National Convention (audio footage).

My Soul Is Rested: Movement Days in the Deep South Remembered
http://www.ala.org/ala/acrl/acrlpubs/crlnews/backissues2004/september04/civilrights.htm

National Civil Rights Museum
http://www.civilrightsmuseum.org/

New York Public Library Schomburg Center for Research in Black Culture
http://www.nypl.org/research/sc/sc.html

Rosa Parks Library and Museum
http://www.tsum.edu/museum/

Rosa Parks: A Woman Who Changed a Nation
http://www.montgomeryadvertiser.com/1news/specialreports/rosa/rosasplash.html

U.S. Department of Justice Civil Rights Division
http://www.usdoj.gov/crt/

Voices of the Civil Rights Era
http://www.webcorp.com/civilrights/voices.htm.
Audio clips of famous people, events, and places.

We Shall Overcome: Historic Places of the Civil Rights Movement
http://www.cr.nps.gov/nr/travel/civilrights/index.htm

We Shall Overcome: The History of the Civil Rights Movement as It Happened
http://www.npr.org/templates/story/story.php?storyId=4193803&sourceCode=RSS
Narrated by Ossie and Ruby Davis.

INDEX

PHOTO CREDITS

ABOUT THE AUTHORS

Sheila Jackson Hardy and P. Stephen Hardy collaborate as writers. Their first collaboration was a children's story on Augusta Savage, a Harlem Renaissance artist. Sheila is a freelance writer and former columnist who has written for *Essence* magazine and other publications.

Stephen is a writer, art historian, art curator, and self-taught artist. His paintings have been featured in galleries throughout the United States. The couple is now working together on a new pr[...] screenplays. They live in Los Angeles, Califo[...]